Paulette F. Ford
Alternative High
School

More Ghostly Tales from Minnesota

Ruth D. Hein

NORTH STAR PRESS OF ST. CLOUD, INC.

This book is dedicated to

THE STORYGIVERS

Front Cover Photos: Cecelia S. Dwyer

Copyright ©August 1999 Ruth D. Hein

ISBN: 0-87839-134-7

2nd Printing, October 2000

Printed in the United States of America by
Versa Press, Inc., of East Peoria, Illinois

Published by
North Star Press of St. Cloud, Inc.
P.O. Box 451
St. Cloud, Minnesoda 56302

Contents

Not Disappointed on Disappointment Lake

WHEN A HIBBING RADIO STATION interviewed me by phone early in 1999 about my ghost stories, Paul Minerich from Hibbing called in to offer a story. A little later, he sent more details.

Paul wrote, "It was on a Thursday morning in May 1995. Four of us had decided to go fishing at Ima Lake in Lake County. We left Snowbank Lake, west of Ima Lake, at about 7:15 that morning."

It was an ideal day, according to Paul's notes. The sky was partly cloudy, and a gentle northwest wind blew, just right for canoeing. About forty-five minutes later, the four had paddled across Snowbank Lake to their first portage.

The guys were all happy to be on their first Boundary Waters canoeing adventure for the season, Paul wrote. They had made a double portage because they had taken along plenty of gear. The portage itself took almost an hour. Once that was accomplished, they headed out of the portage bay and started across Disappointment Lake, a small lake with just thirteen miles of shoreline. By then, the sky had begun to cloud over, and the wind had picked up a little, but it was generally nice for paddling. In fact, Paul wrote, they were all in agreement about one thing: It was such an ideal day that nothing could go wrong.

To set the scene a bit, on a map of the Lake County of northern Minnesota one can find Disappointment Lake among many smaller and larger lakes. Adjoining lakes have even stranger names: Jitterbug Lake, Muzzle

1

Lake, Drumstick Lake, Robe Lake, and Sable Lake. All are nestled among others in just a small part of northern Lake County and within the Boundary Waters Canoe Area. Somewhat larger lakes nearby are Moose Lake, Ensign Lake, and Snowbank Lake.

The four friends figured if they could get to Ahsub Lake before the wind increased, then the rest of the smaller lakes to Jordan Lake would be easier to navigate. Just as their two canoes nosed into the waters of Disappointment Lake, Paul looked across the water toward the far trees and was startled to see a whitish, misty mass there. It was moving quickly up the shoreline in and out of the timber. It wasn't a person. It was bigger. Not a reflection, because clouds shaded that area just then.

Paul called out to the others, "Did you see that thing in the woods?" But it was gone already when they looked. They laughed at him.

What Paul had seen looked big. It reminded him of a small boxcar or maybe even a horse, ridiculous as the comparison seemed. There was no railroad on that strip of land, and as far as he knew, no farm.

Paul continued paddling, but he kept an eye out ahead. Then that same mass appeared again. This time he yelled as he pointed toward it, "Look! There it is again. Over there in the woods! Over there!"

Paul related what happened next. "This time, I was in the front canoe. My partner saw it, too. He asked, 'What on earth is that?' He had no clue, and that bothered him a little. He was the one who always had answers for everything. This time the apparition was nearer the shoreline, and we could see it better. It appeared to be a large, loose mass like a huge white puffball of some kind, or maybe a billowy cloud hanging low over the shore. It made no sound—at least none we could hear from out on the lake, even while we rested our paddles. It hovered just above the shore. As we watched, it shifted direction a little. Then it moved farther along and was suddenly out of sight."

Tim, a friend in the other canoe, said later, "I had no idea what it was, and I still don't!"

Bob, in the canoe with Tim, said, "I was privileged to see whatever it was, when it appeared the third time."

Paul wrote, "We didn't hear from Bruce, though, until we all drew up to the shore near that wooded area, and I will admit, a little apprehensively.

"We were on the shore only a few minutes when he said, 'I don't know what it was, and I don't see it now, so we could examine it if we wanted to, but it clearly, definitely, absolutely was there!'"

The mysterious object or mirage, if it was that, was visible for only about ten seconds, but all four of the men saw it that time. It was about three hundred yards away from them. There was definitely something unusual on the island. According to Paul, the expressions on their faces reflected surprise, puzzlement, disbelief—almost fear.

Paul referred to his canoeing partner as "Mr. College Boy" who "couldn't believe his educated eyes, but had caught a glimpse" of it. Tim thought it was a large animal, maybe a horse, except that as it moved about it took on different shapes, like varied masses of fog he had encountered when driving on a country road in low areas at night. He watched it move quickly and disappear in the woods even as he realized it couldn't be fog; the air was clear.

As they all paddled quietly with the canoes almost side by side, Bob saw something, too—the ghost, apparition, or whatever it was—but he wouldn't say anything. He just wanted to get out of there as fast as he could.

At first, they all had an eerie feeling as they saw this strange thing and then watched it vanish. But Paul soon laughed at the others. He said, "I told you there was something strange over there in the woods. You didn't believe me. But by the way you look now, you must think it was a ghost."

They went on paddling until they reached Ima Lake. That night, on the shore there, they had a tasty fish supper before they sat around their campfire talking over the first day of their adventure. Not much was said about the apparition they had seen on that shoreline. But later on Paul said, "In the quiet of the evening out there on the shore of Ima Lake, I think we all mulled it over in our minds a million times. I don't know what explanation the others came up with—they apparently weren't comfortable talking about it—but I believe an old Indian chieftain's spirit lurks in the timber and roams at will through the wilderness of the great Boundary Waters Canoe Area. I think maybe we came close to meeting him that day. If we were looking for adventure as we crossed Disappointment Lake, we definitely were *not* disappointed."

We Had No Answers

As soon as the Kangas family moved into the house in Cohasset, a few miles northwest of Grand Rapids, things started to happen. Rachel said that, actually, it all started earlier when they were fixing up the house, getting ready to move in. That was during the winter.

Bob and Rebecca, Rachel's parents, were installing paneling in some of the rooms and laying carpeting in others. When they left in the evenings, they always made sure all the doors and windows were closed and locked. They never used the front door, and they didn't even have a key for the lock, so they just left it locked as they had found it.

One day, after having worked there the night before, they went back to the house. There had been a fresh snowfall during the night. Once they were inside, they found that the front door was wide open. On checking, they found no footprints outside that could be considered someone's tracks up to the house. That seemed strange, strange enough that they didn't feel like talking about it.

Once the Kangases moved in, they had to get used to a whole new set of sounds. They accepted that; it was a natural thing that each house had unique sounds— until the sounds and the activity became really weird.

Rachel said, "My mom and dad's bedroom was downstairs, and our rooms were upstairs. My dad, Bob, started hearing footsteps coming down the stairs at night, but none going up. Before we moved into that house, Dad had been a very sound sleeper. But now he

5

would get up to see who came downstairs. There was never anybody down there but Dad and Mom.

"Then something started waking Dad at the odd hour of 12:13 A.M. every night. He would hear a clicking noise in the kitchen. First, he thought it was just the timer or the clock on the stove getting stuck. One night, he stayed up and sat by the stove to watch this happen. After months of being awakened by the strange sound, he really wanted to figure it out. But that night when he kept watch, nothing happened at all, nor did it ever happen again after that night."

Rachel said that sometimes when the family got up in the morning, the door going from the kitchen to the basement would be wide open. Sometimes they could hear it open and close during the night. Rachel recalled, "Dad decided to lean a twenty-pound bag of potatoes against that door before he went to bed, but the door would still open and close or be open in the morning. He put a sliding lock on the door, and it still happened. Sometimes we heard strange sounds like pans rattling when no one was in the kitchen. Sometimes when Natasha, my sister, was upstairs doing homework, she would come down and ask, 'What did you want?' because she had heard someone call her, but none of us had."

In their bathroom was a closet where the family kept supplies like shampoo, soap, towels, cough medicine and other "bathroom stuff." Sometimes when no one was in the bathroom, the closet door would open and all those things would fly off the shelves onto the floor. Rachel's mother saw it happen more than once.

On other occasions, they sometimes heard a baby or even several babies crying when none were present in the house.

Rachel said, "When Mom was very sick and in and out of the hospital in Deer River as well as the one at the University of Minnesota in the Twin Cities and also the Mayo Clinic, she spent a lot of time in bed. One evening as she lay reading, she felt that someone was watching her. She looked up, and there at the foot of the bed she saw an elderly Native American sitting cross legged, dressed in traditional garb—headdress, blanket, and all. He didn't speak, but just sat there. When he smiled at her, Mom looked away, thinking 'I must be dreaming.' When she looked again, he was gone. We always wondered afterward what that had to do with the history of the property.

"Some members of the family felt a cold draft such as one would feel when someone walked by. The air would move, but no one would be there to cause it. That happened a lot in the basement.

"One of the strange features of that basement was that though the floors were cemented, in one corner there was no cement. That space with the dirt floor was about the size of a coffin. The really bad odor down there at times was puzzling because it would be there for a while, but just that fast it would be gone or would change to a more pleasant odor like that of a heady perfume. Our toy poodle, Benji, wouldn't go down into the basement at all; the closest he got was the top of the stairs, where he just sat and growled and barked or sometimes took off yelping as he went to hide in a corner and growl. There seemed to be no reason for that."

Once, when Bob and Rebecca were at a hospital in The Cities, Rachel's aunt stayed with the children. While she was there, she slept in the downstairs bedroom. One night she felt a cold breeze. Suddenly the blankets were jerked off the bed. She knew nothing about the things that had been happening. She lived in Indiana, and no one had told her.

Rachel moved to Grand Rapids after she graduated from high school. She was only five miles from her family when her own son was born on June 27, 1985. On October 22 that fall, he died of sudden infant death syndrome. Rachel moved back home.

Rachel and Vincent, her fiancé, stayed at the house then, using the sofa bed in the living room. One night when everyone else was asleep, they were still watching a movie on TV. Rachel soon fell asleep. Vincent heard a crash in the kitchen. When he checked, he saw nothing that would explain the noise. The next morning, he described the sound "as if someone dropped and spilled a big box of silverware all over the floor." No one else had heard it.

"One morning," Rachel said, "we came into the kitchen to find a buttered piece of bread with one bite out of it on the counter. That was pretty hard to account for, but everyone there said, 'I didn't do it.'"

After Rachel married, she moved to Tennessee. A friend there had a Ouija board. The two of them decided to use it. Rachel had never touched one before that time. She had always considered them just a silly game, so she played. At her turn, she asked, "Is the ghost or spirit that's living in my parents' house just there to have fun?" The answer was "YES." Then her friend told her, "These things sometimes lie." Rachel asked her question again, and the board spelled out "EVIL." That scared Rachel, so she quit playing. Two days later, she had a really bad feeling about her family, so she called home and talked with Rebecca.

Rachel reported, "Mom said things were getting really bad in the house. They were thinking of having the place exorcised. I told her about my playing the Ouija board, and I promised her I would never play it again. About a week later they had a couple of preachers come in. They prayed in each room and over Benji and our cat, Harry, outside, and over everybody in the house. After that, all the scary incidents stopped. My family moved out and rented the house to others, but none of those renters stayed very long. One family said they heard noises they couldn't identify. Another family said the same. Then a family wanted to buy the house. It was even stated in the contract that strange, unexplainable things happened there. The prospective owner said he had heard about that but wasn't worried. He figured it was just wind or a squirrel on the roof or something like that making the noises. He bought it.

Later, Rachel heard that when one of the sons of the new owner came home from school one day and was alone in the house, he went up to his room and found his skis standing straight up as if on end, suspended, not touching the floor. He screamed. They fell. He ran from the house.

When Rachel no longer lived in that house, she heard a little about its earlier history. At one time, it had been used as a day-care facility. During that time, a young child turned up missing and was never found.

Rachel said, "When I told that to my dad, he told me something else very strange. He said, 'Once when I was mowing the yard, I ran over a bump or something. When I started to dig it up to level it off, I found a barrel buried out there. I pried it open and found a pair of baby shoes and some baby clothes on top of whatever else was in there. I didn't look through the rest of the stuff, beyond what I could see in the top of it. I hauled it and its contents to the dump.'"

There was another story Rachel heard about a family that once lived in the house. They had a teen-age boy and a younger girl. When the boy had just gotten his driver's license and a car, he took his sister for a ride. Unfortunately, there was an accident. He rolled the car. His sister was decapitated, according to the story Rachel was told. The young driver lived.

"When we first moved in," Rachel said, "we wondered why some people asked us questions like 'How do you like the house?' or 'Have you heard any strange noises?' or 'Considering all the things that happen there, how can you sleep at night?'

"Well, after we lived there awhile, we could easily have answered those questions and more. But we weren't a bit sure that we had the right answers."

Heinrich Must Have Loved His Place

EVEN AFTER AL RELATED A SERIES of otherwise unexplainable incidents, he said, "I still find it hard to believe there are ghosts . . . yet it's totally baffling when I try to explain what happened. Truthfully, I can tell you what happened, but I can't explain why or how it happened."

Al said some baffling occurrences took place on an old farm near New Ulm through more than a decade . . . specifically, from 1982 to 1994.

That Sunday when Al came to tell his story he started, "First, I must tell you that I bought a burro when the Department of Natural Resources (DNR) made them available in the early 1980s. I figured Milton, as I called him, would make a good lawnmower and save me some work.

"It was through a program by the U.S. Bureau of Land Management, a western states' version of the DNR, that I acquired Milton. It was later found that their diets in this area did not include enough selenium, found more abundantly in desert soil. As a result, rickets or something similar set in after about eighteen months. Local vets didn't recognize the problem. Milton ultimately developed a bad hip, and I developed a good aim.

"I was one of ten children. In May of 1982, I moved from the family farm home to an abandoned farm that had been vacant for ten years. That is, Milton and I moved there.

"The farm was only six miles away from home. I had gone by it many times, and I was always intrigued by the placement of the buildings. They were well secluded from

10

passersby. The building site was quite close to the road, with about a twenty-foot driveway, but set in a dense grove of about eighteen different species of trees. Among others, I remember tamaracks, maples, cedars, a couple of white birch, and one huge old elm. The buildings stood in a clearing, surrounded by all these trees.

"The driveway developed into a cul-de-sac where three tall pines larger than any of the other trees blocked the view of most of the house. The pines are still there.

"I set out to make a sidewalk near the house. As I dug down, I found a sidewalk already there. A retaining wall had been built of grey lava rock. It made an ideal housing for yellow jackets! The old sidewalk led from the existing porch to the retaining wall, exactly where I was preparing to lay one.

"To the right, I had noticed a two- or three-foot mound of dirt. On it were three old cedar trees all tangled together and having the appearance of bonsai-type trees, not much higher than the interior walls of the rooms of a house, but appearing to have been deliberately pruned.

"As I removed the dirt from that mound, I gradually found that it had once held a pond with an island in it. The three tangled cedar trees had grown on the island. The pond had been knee deep, about six feet by three feet oblong, and bordered by rocks.

"Later, I learned from the daughter of Heinrich, the elderly gentleman who had built the pond, that he had collected those rocks from all forty-eight contiguous states. He had also built a concrete, one-foot-wide decorative bridge from the edge of the pond to its center, to the island. Afterward, in the early 1980s, he passed away, leaving his work of art to the elements and to the neglect of others. He was over ninety when he died.

"There, in that secluded setting, was the T-shaped two-story house with wood siding. No attic. Only one small room for a basement. On yard level, the house had an enclosed porch, with a door on the south side. The road ran north and south past the place.

"When I was a kid, I rode by there many times with my folks. For years, I'd had dreams about this house. The seclusion and dark brown colors of the buildings and the shadows of the trees were all elements in those dreams. I would see the house with its east-facing doorway looking out toward the road. In those dreams, I always saw a man in the doorway, looking out toward the road. I'll tell you more about that, later.

"Other significant structures on the farm were a barn, a granary, and a shop. The barn was built into a hillside, with just one long side and one end exposed. A large concrete cistern was near the barn, with more rocks around the cistern for landscaping. There was no lake or creek nearby, so I always wondered if those rocks were painstakingly picked from the fields or if they were also gathered from other places, other states, during Heinrich's travels.

"The wooden granary on a part-stone foundation stood at the highest point of the land. It rested on six boulders at the points of support.

"Not far from the road was a brick building I used for a shop when I lived there. It may once have been a garage, with handy access to the road from where it stood.

"When Milton and I moved in during May of 1982, I had frequently been playing my concertina in a band into the late evening and early morning hours. When I came in at those hours, I was often greeted by the ruckus made by rats and ground squirrels that had taken over while the place was abandoned. They had easy access because the house walls had pushed away about three inches from the field rock foundation. I guess the little critters considered me an intruder, but in reality I had been offered the place rent free just for looking after it.

"I learned that Heinrich, the old gent who had worked so hard to beautify the grounds, had hired transient painters to paint the house for him in the early

1960s. When they sprayed white paint on the house, the overspray also covered the screens, windows, and even the fuel barrel braced against the side of the house. Everything was white for a while then."

While Heinrich lived there, he apparently also used the house for storage. When Al moved in, there were boards, front-end tractor tires, and other items leaning against the inner walls. That didn't bother Milton, of course, and neither did all the debris in the yard. Milton just nosed around through it. But Al had to clear out a lot of things before he could be comfortable indoors.

As he went on with his story, Al said, "I first occupied the main-floor living room as my bedroom, for about five years. Then I moved to the upstairs for sleeping quarters. The rooms up there were dirty, but completely empty when I cleaned them and moved up.

"But that first year, I didn't like to go upstairs very much. After moving into the house in May 1982, I just wasn't at ease up there. Maybe it had something to do with what happened on July first, when I was still sleeping on an old army cot on first floor. I was awakened that night by sounds as if someone was bouncing a basketball upstairs, except it must have been much heavier . . . more like a bowling ball. It hit so hard on the floor up there that it knocked chips of paint and filler from the joints in the plywood ceiling down in the living room.

"That scared me so much that I ran outside to compose myself. Then I thought maybe one of my friends was just trying to scare me, but I remembered that none of my friends knew yet that I was living there. Besides, I couldn't think of anyone who would do that. When I went back in, the sounds had stopped and a quick check showed there was no one else in the house. I decided to just let it be. What else could I do? But I didn't forget about it.

"Through the rest of that summer, nothing else strange happened, except that outside, usually in the daytime but also twice at night, as I went from the yard project to the shop for another piece of equipment or whatever, I felt that I had brushed up against something. That happened ten or twelve times, always on my left side. No, it wasn't Milton bumping against me. It was just a gentle brushing, as when you brush up against some curtains or drapes, or outside against clothes on the lines. Sometimes it felt harder, as when you collide with someone. But there was never anyone there—not even Milton. I always checked, and usually found him out by the granary. Once, there was so much impact that it made me dizzy, and I walked around that particular spot in a three-foot circle before I went on, pretending nothing had happened. Twice that summer, in the early morning hours after I came home from playing in the band, I felt a lighter brushing, and I just went on my way into the house, trying to pretend it didn't happen.

"One night I found myself anticipating the brushing, but it didn't happen. I kept my head down as I went up the two steps in the retaining wall, going toward the house. Then I looked up to see someone above the flat porch roof. I had almost known it beforehand, when I felt as if I was being watched. That was the only time anything actually appeared. What I saw was not silhouetted against the house, but against the southwestern sky. The figure's head was fairly large, with no hat or cap, but it wore an overcoat. It had no feet or legs; there was nothing between the hem edge of the overcoat and the porch roof below it. Uncanny as that was, I didn't let it bother me. Maybe I was getting used to these incidents . . . or maybe I was tired from the job and the late hour. I fell asleep easily.

"Nothing else happened until late the next spring, when the frost had gone out of the ground, leaving it a little spongy. When I left the house, going down the two steps into the cul-de-sac at the end of the sidewalk, I suddenly jumped up as quickly as a cat sometimes springs up from its resting place. There was a person's arm, with a kid's watch on the wrist, lying there on the ground. I looked again, and I saw it about three times in that same place before I turned away. When I turned back to look once more, it was gone.

"There were more 'arm' and 'hand' appearances. One night in 1983 or 1984, our band played at Arlington, about thirty-two miles northeast of New Ulm. We were leaving Arlington on the first curve in the road south of town. I was driving myself and three other band members in my Suburban and towing the band trailer. I veered sharply to the right to avoid an arm lying in the road . . . again, with a watch around the wrist. I came to an abrupt stop, made a U-turn, and said to the guys, 'You've gotta see this!' I drove back about 150 feet but didn't see the arm anywhere. The guys didn't see it, either. What was worse, they ridiculed me. But I felt goosebumps for quite a while as we rode on home.

"In August of 1984, my eleven-year-old son, Russ, from my first marriage was visiting me on the farm as he often did during the summers. This time, he wanted to stay overnight. He didn't know about the incidents. I kept them to myself, I was so puzzled about them. So I said, 'Sure. You can sleep upstairs on the army cot.'

"At 11:30 that evening, he was awakened by buzzing sounds. Through the closed door, he hollered out, 'Dad! Dad, come up here, and bring the fly spray with you. The buzzing of all those flies out in the hall is keeping me awake.'

"I answered, 'Yep! I'll bring it. Comin' right up!' knowing full well there were no flies. I must have sprayed half a can of fly spray to satisfy Russ. As I went back down, I called out, 'There! That ought to take care of 'em!'

"The next morning at breakfast, Russ asked, 'Where did all the flies go? Were there a lot? I didn't see any on the hall floor just now.'

"I just overlooked his question and served him breakfast.

"In 1984, the rest of us were leaving for a short vacation. We would be gone for a week and a half, so I asked

Russ to stay there on the farm during that time. He agreed. He knew nothing of what had gone on there. I'd never mentioned those scary happenings to him.

"Many months later, when I went to visit Russ, he told me that when we were gone that time, he only stayed there twice at night. After the second night, he only stayed there in the daytime. On the other nights, he stayed in town.

"I asked him what happened that second night. He told me that he decided to have a party that night. He had fifteen to eighteen friends come out. I suppose they smoked, drank beer, whatever kids did then when they partied while the adults weren't around. But the kids kept commenting on how weird the place was. Something was spooking them, so they moved the party from the house out to the barn. By midnight, only a few kids were left, and Russ sensed something, too, so that's why he stayed in town the other nights.

"Later, when he met up with some of those same kids again, they told him they left because they thought the place was real spooky.

"Things were rather quiet then during the rest of 1984. My wife-to-be moved in with me, and our child was born May 30, 1985. But shortly before her birth, there was another incident.

"I am an avid motorcyclist as are some of my close friends. In the middle of that May, two of those close friends were riding their cycles in a group of about eight when they were involved in an accident at Morgan, northwest of New Ulm. One was in serious condition at St. Mary's Hospital in Rochester. One, who was flown to another hospital, died in mid-May as a result of the accident. Then came May 21, 1985.

"At the time, our bedroom was still in the downstairs living room, though I had moved the old army cot to an upstairs room by then. I was awakened by loud pounding on the inside front door, inside the enclosed porch, at 8:00 A.M. I hollered, 'Yah . . . I'm coming!' I sat on the edge of the bed, pulling on my trousers, when the loud knocking was repeated. I shouted again, 'I'm coming!' My wife woke up and asked, 'What are you doing? Where are you going?'

"I said, 'There's someone at the door.'

"She said, 'No, there's not!'

"Well, I went to the front door anyway and pulled the green curtains aside, but there wasn't anyone there. I asked, 'Who's there?' Then I heard a voice say, somewhat as a question, 'Al?' I recognized the voice immediately. I said, 'Vernie!' Then the voice asked, 'Al, can I come in?' It was the voice of the friend who had died in the accident on May 19th. As I let go of the curtains, I felt a serious case of goosebumps. I remember stepping back half a step, enough for the door to clear when I opened it farther. Then I looked into the enclosed porch area, but no one was there. I stepped out into the porch, but still didn't see anyone out there. When I went to the door to the outside and opened it, I saw to my left a semi tractor and flatbed trailer parked facing west, with about thirty feet between its front bumper and the house. It was my friend Vernie's truck. I was astounded!

"As I stared at it, Mary Lou called out from the house, 'Who's there?'

"I turned to see if she was near enough so I could show her the truck. She wasn't there at all. She had stayed in bed.

"When I turned back, the semi was gone. I stood there staring and scratching my head, totally perplexed. Vernie was dead, but his voice and his truck seemed so very real that night.

"It was about ten days later that our baby girl was born. At Christmas time that year, she was seven months old. We didn't have running water. We had to get water from outside and heat it inside to wash the diapers. Mary Lou was facing the wall, washing diapers with the help of a wringer washer, while I sat across the room facing her, rocking our daughter. Suddenly little Erin shuddered, causing me to hold her closer. I suspected what it was, but I watched her head turn as she followed 'it.' Out of the corner of my eye I saw what looked like rippling rays of sunlight shining through a mist or a fog.When it reached the stove, the baby's rattle fell to the floor, confirming that what Erin saw was whatever had also drawn my attention many times.

"There was another hand and arm incident in 1987. I came upon the site of an accident that had apparently just happened. No one was there yet to help or to investigate. On I-80 near mile marker 180 or 190, I was driving my semi when I stopped where two cars were on the right shoulder and a pickup with its windshield broken out was in the median. You see, on weekends I played in the band. On week days, I drove a truck.

"As I looked around in the median near the truck, I went on looking around in the tall, unmowed grass. It hadn't been mowed for quite a while because this was a road construction zone. With the help of my flashlight, I first saw a reflection from a watch on an arm. I felt goosebumps again. Then I shone my flashlight into the tall grass to look beyond the arm, to find the body of the twelve-year-old boy who had died in the accident, as I learned later.

"In June of 1988, after I spent some weeks, maybe months, of thought on whether I should spend any time or money improving the house, I saw an ad in the local paper advertising a picture window in good condition. The party offered to give it away. I thought, 'Here in the kitchen, these two old-style upright windows face the yard and driveway. I could take them out and put in a picture window instead. That would be a good place for one.'

"I took some measurements where the window would be, picked up the free window unit, and took it out to the farm. One day, a little later, I thought, 'This is it! I'm gonna put that window in! I'll put some time into the house for once.'

"Inside the kitchen, I cleared things out of the way. I measured again where the window would be, and this time I snapped the chalkline there. My intentions were that instead of removing layer by layer of paneling, plaster, laths, oak frames, and exterior siding, I would use my chain saw. I always kept it sharp and ready because we cut a lot of wood for heating the house. If cutting through the nails and plaster ruined the chain, I'd just toss it and buy a new one. The old one was getting worn anyhow.

"I went to the shop to get the chain saw, but it wasn't there. It was still good . . . a Stihl, practically new . . . but it was not on its shelf. Then I thought, Bummer! Russ must have borrowed it. I got in touch with him. He said, 'No, Dad, I haven't used it for a long time.' I knew then that he was telling the truth because it had always been right there in its place in the shop when I wasn't using it myself.

"In the meantime, I had a phone call. A construction firm in New Ulm had contracted to build a new Super 8 Motel on the south end of town. There was a huge grove of cottonwoods on the site . . . about a whole square block of 'em. The person who called said, 'Come and get 'em. If you cut 'em down, you can have 'em.'

"I thought I'd better get at it if I wanted the wood. If I didn't, if someone else would take it on, I'd be out of all that fuel. I decided to let the window job wait until later. I got all worked up about it and the fact that I couldn't find the chain saw, which I would need desperately to cut down all those trees. In the shop, I sat down on my son's snowmobile. I thought, Where can that thing be? I couldn't figure it out. I decided to drive into town and buy a new one; the trees would be worth that much. I went out by the big sliding door and got in my car to go to town. The last minute, I thought, I'll just have one more quick look. So I ran inside through the side door, flicked on the light, and there that chain saw was, sitting right there on the seat of the snowmobile, where I had been sitting thirty seconds before! That really made me feel shaky!

"Well, I did get the cottonwoods cut down and eventually cut up into firewood lengths. And I did put the picture window in before winter. But as I look back, it seems that every time I was planning to do some work that would make changes on the house, little incidents like this one would occur, as if someone didn't want me to change the status quo of the place.

"Please keep in mind that, sometimes, when I felt that something was going to happen, it disoriented me. In 1990 my son Brad, who was twenty-two then, had a well-trained black Lab hunting dog called Chester. Chester obeyed Brad to a "T." The two of them came to visit. Brad and I were sitting in front of the brick farm shop out toward the road, talking about going past the stand of trees and on out to the ditch to shoot at anything that moved.

"When Brad said, 'Let's go!' I had a queazy feeling. I let him go ahead. Seeing that the dog didn't follow, Brad said, 'Here, Ches!' Ches didn't respond. I began to follow Brad, even knowing something was amiss. Chester must have sensed that, too. Brad kept on walking, with me following him, watchful. Suddenly Brad wavered a little. A few seconds later, he reached the road shoulder. When I reached the spot where he had faltered, I immediately found myself taking a wide stance to stabilize myself. I felt a little dizzy or disoriented again, walking through the same spot. We both looked back toward the shop, and this time, Ches started toward us. When he reached that same spot, he cowered and made a half circle before he came toward us on the road shoulder. We went down the road to the ditch. Brad was unaware of the previous incidents on that farm site. He stopped, looked me in the eye at arm's length, and said, 'Dad, did I ever get dizzy back there!' I let the conversation end right there. I made no comment at all.

"A couple of years later . . . in fact, on the first of April, 1992 . . . I was sitting outside in a lawn chair about 10:30 on a beautiful sun-shiny morning. The kids and their mother had gone into town.

"The chair was in the driveway, but about halfway in the doorway of the shop. I was leaning back, relaxed, a can of pop in hand, and I was watching the little bonfire I had going. I was burning scraps from the table saw in the shop. I must have dozed off a bit, or else something made me go into a daze. As I came to again, I put my head back and sensed a big, black car pulling in. I didn't really see it, but I knew it was there. I dozed off again, and the next thing I knew, someone was saying, 'Al! Wake up!'

"I opened my eyes and there, to my right, stood a man. I recognized the well-known orchestra leader known to many in the area as Guy. He said, 'Al, come with me to the feed house in the barn. You've been having some trouble with an outlet there.'

"The kids and I were raising some chicks in the feedhouse. And, yes, we were having trouble with an outlet. The heat lamp came on only when it wanted. The two of us went to the barn, but on the way there I had no sense of walking. It was more like I was gliding along beside him. When we got there, he said, 'Your problem is here in this receptacle. Pull it out. The wire's attached, but there's a break in the wire just a couple inches from where it's attached to the receptacle.'

"I went to the shelf in the feedhouse where I kept a few tools handy. Picking up a screwdriver, I moved on to the problem. Using the screwdriver, I proceeded to fix the receptacle, still not feeling fully aware. Suddenly I realized he wasn't there any more. I looked around and I called out, 'Guy! Where are you?' I was totally confused. I put the screwdriver down, went back to the shop, and sat down again in the lawn chair. I wondered, *Is my mind leaving me, or what?*

"The next thing I knew, my wife was standing there asking, 'What's wrong, Al? Are you all right? Wake up! Can you hear me?'

She must have thought I'd had a stroke or a heart attack or something.

After a little bit, she said, 'I'm going to call the emergency room.' She went to the house. I wanted to tell her I was fine, but I couldn't speak. The next minute, she was out there again saying, 'Why don't you come to the house and lie down a while . . . take a little nap. Rest up.'

"I got up. We walked to the house together. But, again I couldn't feel myself walking. It seemed that if she had touched me, I wouldn't have felt it. I wasn't responsive at all. Then she went ahead of me up the steps to the sidewalk, where she turned around and asked, 'This is no April Fool's joke, is it?'

"I wanted to tell her, 'I wish it was,' but it wasn't.

"My next recollection of time was about 4:30 that afternoon, when I woke up and everything seemed fine. Two days later, I heard a funeral notice on the radio. It was for my friend Guy, the man who had been on the farm two days earlier. Guy was older, in his mid-seventies. He was the son-in-law of the woman who owned the farm then. He had married her daughter. I found out later that he had been sick for a long time and had been confined to an upstairs apartment, not capable of driving or walking. He was on oxygen, and he was bedridden. How could that be? How could he have been out there on the farm that day, helping fix things? I can't figure it out.

"In November 1994, our family moved to our present home in New Ulm. I had already owned that place and had been using it for rental income while I lived on the old farm, rent free.

"At Christmas time, the furnace motor went out in that house in town. On installing a spare motor I had on hand, I found that the adjustable pulley didn't fit. I remembered I had one on the farm, and I knew just where it was, on a shelf in the shop. It had been there for years. I had never moved it, though I had taken many other items from that shop into town when we moved and later, as the need arose.

"I went out to get that pulley. The headlights of my Blazer were shining into the side shop door, but I needed more light, so I put the fuses back into the fusebox on the yardlight pole before I entered the shop. I went right to the workbench shelf where the pulley was. I got up on the workbench and checked the upper shelf. Meanwhile, under the workbench was a big, copper wastebasket in which there was something . . . maybe a rat or a muskrat . . . clawing to get out. I knelt down on the workbench, leaned over, and pulled the basket out. There was nothing in it. I shoved it back, looked for the pulley, and the clawing sound continued. I checked the waste basket again. Nothing there, but goosebumps on my arms again. I pulled it out once more. Nothing, again! Within seconds, I felt fear . . . serious panic . . . setting in. I thought, *I gotta find that pulley and get outta here.* I stood up again. I felt the metal pulley next to my shoe even as I heard the klink a metal pulley would make when it was set down there. I was becoming almost rigid with fright. I don't remember jumping off the bench, but I remember running out of the shop, hopping into the Blazer, putting it in reverse and backing up over a pile of castiron radiators and getting the Blazer hung up there. I remember telling myself to calm down and rock the Blazer. I got it off the pile okay. On my way back to town, I stopped at a friend's place to collect my senses. He asked, 'Al, do you want a beer or somethin'?' I guess he saw that I was totally white. He asked, 'What's wrong?'

I said, 'Nothing. I'll just take the beer.' And I never did tell him about this weird experience I had looking for that pulley in the shop. And that was the last time I set foot on that farm, after thirteen years living there.

"No one lived on that old farm for a couple of years after I left it. In 1996 the house was demolished by a contracting firm. The new owners of the property were planning to build a new house on the place. I happened to drive by there in my Blazer while the old house was being taken down. I saw a backhoe scraping off the siding. I stopped to watch. No, I didn't get out of my Blazer. I felt secure as long as I stayed in it.

"As I watched, a door and doorway appeared in the demolition. It was like the one I had always seen in my childhood dreams. The door had been, briefly, an east-facing doorway, but it had always been hidden by the siding when I looked toward the house as we passed by in recent years. All those years I lived there, I thought it wasn't the house in my dreams that had an east-facing doorway, when, in fact, it was, but the original doorway had been hidden, perhaps to block the view of passers-by.

"I wish I could say Milton was responsible for all these strange happenings, but I'm afraid that would be burdening him with just too much responsibility. Besides, he died before I left the farm. Let's let him rest in peace."

Deceased Boxer Still Works Out in the Gym

THE MOVIE INDUSTRY LOVES using meat lockers and frozen food plants for mysterious or villainous events.

Old meat plants often have a number of rooms, each with a heavy steel door. To that scene is added the numerous sturdy beams supporting the roof or an upper story.

Jim Glancey's Gym, located in a former meat plant at the corner of Beech and Forest in St. Paul's East Side, had hung punching bags on the heavy beams, replacing the sides of beef that once hung there when the brick building housed the Anderson Meat Company.

Aspiring boxers used those punching bags to work out, as a rule in the daytime. They have also been used quite recently by a fighter named Clyde Mudgett. But Mudgett, whom Glancey calls "Mutt," died in 1983.

Mutt's death was rather bazaar. Staff Columnist Don Boxmeyer's story in the May 14, 1996, *St. Paul Pioneer Press* told it in detail. Briefly, here is what happened to make a ghost of the Mutt:

A person called the Anderson Meat Company on a Tuesday in 1983 to report that someone had tried to burglarize the place the previous Sunday. What's more, the caller said that the person might still be in the building, maybe in the chimney!

Sure enough, when the police checked out the plant, they found a suspicious-looking rope tied to the top of a steel ladder attached to the outside of the plant's chimney. But the rope, hanging down into the chimney, apparently hadn't been long enough for what the person

25

who attached it had in mind. Inside the chimney, at the other end of the rope, the police found Clyde Mudgett. He hung about twenty feet up from the floor. After hanging there for three days, he was quite dead. Apparently, besides miscalculating the length of rope he needed, he hadn't correctly figured the interior measurements of the chimney or the size of the clean-out opening at the bottom. He not only didn't make his exit by way of the clean-out as he might have planned, but his body was so firmly lodged in the chimney that the firemen had to chop a hole in the chimney to get the body out.

According to Boxmeyer's story, that wasn't Mudgett's first time in trouble. He already had spent some time in a reformatory. But this time, after his burglary attempt failed and his body was found, he spent a long time confined to a coffin and a grave, all for nothing. Owners of the meat plant said there had been nothing there worth stealing anyway.

Mutt's record, as the police knew it, wasn't his only one. He also had a professional record as a boxer, even including Madison Square Garden and national TV. His great failing, however, was that he didn't like to train.

Jim Glancey, who, at the time of this writing, owned Glancey's Gym—the former meat company building— says, "But now he's making up for that. He (Mutt) works out in my gym, usually at night. And from the sounds I hear when I'm spending what I hoped would be a quiet evening in my rooms on the second floor, I know he's really going at it down there. He has certain favorite punching bags, and at least one of them is right below my rooms!"

Now remember, Mutt is good and dead! Who could be working out in the gym other than Clyde Mudgett's ghost?

"... And You Will Find My Body ..."

MINNESOTA. THE LAND OF 10,000 LAKES. The land of the Dahkotas. The land of the sky-tinted water. Birthplace of many rivers flowing in all directions. Land of prairie, forest, bluff, and waterfall.

Edward D. Neill used such phrases to describe this state, in his *History of Minnesota*. Minnesota, where seventy persons died in the blizzard of 1873.

Southwest Minnesota. "The dark days," "the calamitous days." Land of grasshopper invasions, land of fierce blizzards, according to Arthur P. Rose in his *An Illustrated History of Nobles County, Minnesota* (1908). In Nobles County, four persons died in the blizzard of 1873.

That was a terrible storm, recorded at Fort Snelling as the most violent in the northwest in fifty years. The temperature stayed at about eighteen below zero during all three days of the storm.

John Weston was one of the four victims who died in Nobles County. He was a farmer in Seward Township in the northern part of the county and just west of Graham Lakes Township.

On the morning of January 7, Weston left for Graham Lakes to get a load of wood. It was a beautiful morning for early January. Because of the nice weather, many farmers in the area either had gone to visit their neighbors or left for town for flour or some other necessity. On his way home, although the day had started out clear and mild, Weston was caught in the storm that hit around noon like a great white wall coming down from the northwest.

27

Trying to get home in the blinding storm, he missed his house even though he drove his sled and oxen across his own land, as the tracks showed later. He circled twice, then went more northward, back into Graham Lakes Township. There, Rose's history tells it, he "unhitched and abandoned his ox team, and the animals, after wandering a while, turned the yoke and choked to death. They were found later on the bank of Jack Creek."

Apparently Weston then walked with the storm, toward Hersey (now Brewster, a town just a few miles south of the two Graham Lakes and about eight miles northeast of Worthington).

After he walked about twelve miles, Weston fell on his face in the snow and long grass. But, of course, that wasn't immediately known. The storm was so severe that for three days searchers had to wait for it to die down. When they could finally safely look for John Weston, they found the sled and oxen but went home toward evening without finding their owner. The next April, after the snow had melted, another search party successfully found the body.

So far, the story is straight history recorded in several published references. But this tale also developed into a well-known ghost story, retold by A.P. Miller in *The Worthington Advance* of January 13, 1881, eight years after the blizzard.

D.J. Cosper, a good friend of Weston's, had been a member of the first search party, which had been unable to locate Weston. Later that day, Cosper was feeding his livestock. He came out of the stable to get water for his horses. About half way down the slope to the well, he saw John Weston coming up the path from the creek. It was so natural, he didn't think a thing about it at first. Weston was wearing his blue soldier's overcoat he usually wore in cold weather. He greeted Cosper with his usual greeting, "How goes it?"

Cosper's answer was, "Why, Weston, I thought you were frozen to death!"

Weston answered, "I am, and you will find my body a mile and a half northwest of Hersey." Then he was gone.

After a while, as Mr. Cosper went on about his chores, he realized he had seen a ghost. He told the story to others, and people believed he told the truth. There was no reason to make up such a story about his long-time friend.

Weston's ghost also appeared to his wife. Mary Weston told it this way:

"On the second night of the storm, I heard a knock at the door. I dozed off again. Then I heard a second knock. Over the noise of the wind and sifting snow, I shouted, 'What do you want?' Someone said, 'Did you know that John was frozen to death?' The voice sounded like my brother's. Our son heard it, too, and said from his bed, 'Mother, did Uncle say Pa was frozen to death?'"

Mrs. Weston went to the door then, but no one was out there, and she found no fresh tracks in the snow. When others checked with her brother, a Mr. Linderman, he said he had not been at the Weston home that night. Those who heard Mary's story thought that John Weston wanted to let his family know of his death without frightening his wife, so he made his plight known through the voice of his brother-in-law.

As recorded, when the snow melted in April 1873, John Weston's body was found, just where his ghost said he would be—a mile and one-half northwest of Hersey, near a slough, where the snow had been deep for those three long months.

A Protective Spirit

SOMETHING UNUSUAL HAPPENED a few years ago in an old farmhouse near St. Peter. The woman who told this story has moved to another state, but she's still wondering about the incident.

She said, "I think there is a good spirit walking the earth whom I credit with saving my life!"

Janeen went on to tell what had happened to her. "I was going down the stairs to the main floor one night," she said, "when I started to trip. At the same time, it seemed as if something or someone gently brushed by me and said, 'That's what happened to me.' It was more a thought or a mind message and not a definite audible voice. I didn't fall. I was a little shook up, but I was okay.

"I didn't think much about the incident until the next day when I was telling my fourteen-year-old daughter, Trish, about it. Trish listened at first, then looked as if she were about to interrupt. I said, 'What?' and Trish said, 'Mom, this is really weird! The very same thing happened to me awhile back. It was sort of scary, and I didn't tell anyone. I was afraid you'd think I was making it up. But it made me wonder if something unearthly would happen to one of us.'

"I asked Trish to tell me exactly what had happened. She told me, 'I was going downstairs one night a couple of weeks ago. It was so hot in my room that night! I started down for a glass of cold milk. Just about halfway down, someone or something went by me but didn't say anything. I had the feeling it was a woman, but it wasn't you or Sandi or anyone I know.'"

30

Both mother and daughter kept these occurrences in mind, though they didn't say anything to anyone else. About two years later, Janeen was having trouble with hemorrhaging. One afternoon about four o'clock, she called her doctor, who said he was about to leave his office. But he listened, asked a few questions, and ended the conversation with, "Call me if you have more trouble."

That night, not long before midnight, Janeen woke up to see a woman standing in the doorway of her room. "It wasn't either of the girls. She looked older. She stood there framed by the doorway in a filmy, flowing gown. She was beckoning to me. She wasn't talking but just stretching out a hand and arm toward me, motioning me to get out of bed and come to her. I didn't feel like getting up, but the woman kept on coaxing me, until I actually did get out of bed more out of curiosity than anything.

"As soon as I did, my concern was for myself and my condition. I realized I was hemorrhaging badly. I forgot all about the ghost or spirit or whatever had been compelling me to get up."

Today Janeen says, "I didn't know then what it was all about, but if that hadn't happened—and if I hadn't gotten up to see who or what she was—I might not have known how serious the bleeding was. I called the doctor again, and then Sandi drove me to the hospital where I got the help I needed, and my condition improved."

The next time the three discussed the incidents on the stairs and in Janeen's bedroom, they realized that there was a ghost in their home. They had accepted her by then as a good ghost. She was, in their opinion, the spirit of a woman who had long ago tripped on the stairs and who had come back to protect the later occupants, at least the women, from falling all the way down the stairs or in any other way ending their time on earth prematurely.

This is what she must have meant with her message, "That's what happened to me."

Consider the Consequences

A STORY TOLD BY A NIECE AND NEPHEW of their uncle describes an event that happend sixty years earlier.

The nephew began the story. He said, "My Uncle Bucky, as we knew him, and his friend Tom lived on farms about half a mile apart, between Worthington and Pipestone, about thirty miles from Pipestone on the old diagonal road. For many years earlier, the house on Uncle Bucky's farm had been a stagecoach stop between the two towns. The old diagonal used to go all the way to Pipestone.

"Every oldtimer in the area knew that several Indian burials had taken place on the farm. There were a couple of graves just east of the house, where two Indians killed in a fight were buried right on the spot—probably in the late 1800s. There were never any grave markers, but a clump of cottonwood trees was supposed to mark their location. There may also have been another Indian grave a little farther away.

"My uncle," the nephew continued, "was a bachelor, and he did like to party now and then. One night, Uncle Bucky and his friend Tom, who worked on the next farm, had a few beers at Bucky's house. A few hours and a few more beers later, they were pretty well boozed up. Not realizing what they were doing, and without thinking about the consequences, the two of them started out toward the burial spot. They hoped to find some artifacts or jewelry or something of value in those old graves. To make matters worse, when they got there, they were inebriated enough to relieve themselves on the graves . . .

32

perhaps not intentionally, but of necessity at that moment and place.

"Well, they dug up the graves but found nothing of value—just some old bones. So they chopped up the bones with their shovels, threw the fragments back into the graves, and covered them with the dirt again."

The niece picked up the story. She said, "Those two had always planned to look for valuables there. That night, they had enough guts, or whatever it was, to try it. When they dug down and found clay, they were sure they had the right spot."

Her brother explained, "Farmers pretty easily recognize that wherever the soil is of a different character, like rocks or clay in an otherwise fertile soil, chances are something was buried there. The clay from deeper down would be the last to be turned up to the surface, and the first to be shoveled in again. They had the right spot, all right."

After filling in the graves again, the two men picked up their shovels and somehow found their way to their homes before morning. There they apparently slept off their stupor and their disappointment in not finding anything of value on their "treasure hunt."

For them, life went on as before for a few days. Less than a week later, though, Bucky was suddenly tumbled out of his bed by noises he heard in the night: rattling windows, foundation stones falling out of the walls down in the cellar, dishes and glass jars and crocks falling from the pantry shelves. He thought there was an earthquake.

Bucky didn't know what was happening, and he was frightened. He went over to the farm where Tom worked. Tom said, "I have no idea what brought it on, but the same thing happened to me!"

They checked out the timing and found that the same thing had happened to each of them at the identical time on the same night almost a week after they had visited the graves. That shook them up a bit.

Too afraid to stay in his house alone, Bucky stayed with relatives for a week. All anyone could figure out was that the spirits of the dead had been angered at what had been done to the graves and the remains in them and had shown their displeasure on that night.

Bucky and his relatives decided to ask the priest to go out to the farm to bless the house, grounds, and the graves to rid them of the spirits that must have been taking out their wrath on the two men. That done, Bucky moved back home. About ten years later, other relatives lived there, but nothing so unusual happened. In fact, nothing like that has ever happened since then on that farm.

A Ghost Causes an Accident

CEMETERIES CAUSE SOME PEOPLE to have creepy feelings; other people feel quiet and reflective when they walk through one. Some people have been known to vandalize graveyards. They tip over loose headstones—those tall, old ones not cemented to a heavy, broader base. Some people, on the other hand, find cemeteries fascinating and are often seen searching the records on the markers, seeking out some historical or genealogical detail.

As a youngster, when we passed a cemetery while driving with my family in Dad's old green 1928 Chevy, I liked to make the dry remark, "This is sure a dead part of town." It was a game between my siblings and me to see who could say it first.

Poets have observed that the burial ground really belongs to the dead, as in Kenneth Fearing's "Thirteen O'clock" where the buried ones say, "Go away, live people, stop haunting the dead."

In the story "Over the Fence and Out" in my *Ghostly Tales of Iowa* (1996), a young boy is badly frightened by a three-eyed ghost in a cemetery. Perhaps his older brothers and their friend had played a prank on Robbie.

I have never heard of an adult being as frightened by a cemetery incident, however, as the woman who told this story.

"It happened in Cottonwood County," she said, "at a cemetery close to the road.

"Everyone for miles around knew unpredictable old Hank, who had lived in the area all his life. Everyone had read about him in the papers when he'd killed himself

35

several years earlier. That was a well-known fact. Everyone knew, too, that he'd been buried in that cemetery along the main road.

"Don't ask me what I was thinking about that day. I just don't know. But as I drove past the cemetery in broad daylight, something made me glance up. There was old Hank, leaning against a tree. He was staring at the inscription on one of those huge, white bronze monuments in the section where all the older graves are, down along the road fence.

"I knew Hank had been dead awhile. But there he was! As I tried to cope, my mind did a flip-flop and so did my car. I was so scared that I let go of the steering wheel and my car went into the ditch. When I came to, Hank was gone. Don't think I didn't have a hard time explaining why my car was in the ditch!"

Tim's Guardian Angel

WHEN A FAMILY LIVES IN A HOUSE, and a ghost lives there, too, but only one member of that family is chosen as the one to see the ghost, perhaps there is a reason . . . known only to the ghost! Perhaps there is a special connection or attachment that could suggest the reason for the ghost being so selective.

When this incident happened, the family of five living in a small brown one-story house at 154 Twelfth Street in Windom consisted of Robert and Phyllis Heinitz and their sons Tim, Tom, and Marc. At the time of this writing, Robert and Phyllis still live there, along with the ghost.

The ghost, Marc says, has appeared only twice and only to Tim, the oldest of the brothers. Both times, it showed up after Tim had returned from a considerable length of time spent somewhere else.

The ghost first appeared in 1987 after Tim came home for the summer from his freshman year of college at Mankato State University. He had unpacked and settled into his old room in the basement. He was relaxing one evening when he somehow became aware that someone else was there, too. At first, he thought it was his girlfriend. When "she" came nearer to his bed and gave the covers a little tug, he realized it wasn't anyone he knew.

Raising his head for a better look, Tim asked, "Who are you? What do you want?" He got no response at all. In fact, whoever or whatever he had seen promptly disappeared into the closet. When he overcame his surprise a bit, he looked in the closet—but no one was there, and there was no way any normal living being could have gone anywhere else from there.

Tim had plenty of time to puzzle about what had happened, but it wasn't easy to come up with an answer. He told his brothers about the incident, but they vowed they hadn't seen or heard anything unusual. They also assured him that neither of them was in the house at the time.

In 1988, Tim spent the summer in Alaska working at a fly-in fishing resort. The ghost appeared the first night he was back home from there. It was late in August, and he was asleep in his room with Marc's dogs, Rainy and Trapper, asleep by his side. Perhaps there was a sound. Tim wasn't sure what woke him, but he found the ghost in his room again. It wasn't standing on the floor, but seemed to be floating or hovering above the couch about fifteen feet from his bed.

Startled by what he saw and finding it hard to believe he was actually seeing a shadowy figure hovering in his room, Tim sat up in bed. Again he asked, "Who are you? What do you want? What are you doing here?" He was fully awake by then. He sat there petting Rainy and Trapper, though they were still sound asleep and apparently not in the least disturbed.

When Tim told Marc about the incident, Marc asked, "What did it look like?"

Tim said, "Well . . . it looked kind of like a girl, but she was all in white. She had on some kind of long, filmy dress or gown. And her hair was white, too, and it was really long."

"Did she look young or old?" Marc asked.

"It's funny," Tim began. "I don't know. The outline of the whole figure of a person was there, but there wasn't any face. Come to think of it, I didn't see any feet, either, as she hovered there."

"Were you scared?"

After a moment Tim said, "No, I wasn't really scared. More surprised, at first. Besides, the ghost—if that's what it was—vanished after just fifteen or twenty seconds. When it did, it left me with a peaceful, calm feeling. And that's real strange, considering."

Marc wasn't ready to let the story end there. He asked, "Where did it go? Did it float into the closet again?"

"No. And this is hard to believe, but it floated out between two of the studs, as if there wasn't even a wall there."

To this date, both Tim and Marc end this story with a shiver when they tell it to others. Neither Marc nor Tom, the middle brother, has seen the ghost. But they evidently believe Tim, because neither of them will sleep downstairs when they visit home. Even Tim, who later married, has a hard time convincing his wife Karie to sleep downstairs in his old room when they go to visit, even if the last time Tim saw the ghost was in the summer of 1988.

The ghost has never been anything but friendly. Since none of the family members have heard that earlier residents died in the house or had lost a loved one there or met with a tragic or traumatic death, they think their ghost is Tim's special angel, a guardian angel. They think she was there to make sure he was home and safe after those two long absences.

More Than a Rocking Chair

A COUPLE AND THEIR SEVEN CHILDREN, ages twelve on down, moved to a rambling farm south of Ortonville. In the living room of the two-story house, they found an old wicker rocking chair left by previous occupants. Only that. They thought about throwing it out, but there was something comfortable about its look. It belonged.

The first day was a busy one, but the children found time to explore each room on the main floor, all five bedrooms upstairs, and (on the pretense of needing to carry down the fruit jars and crocks) even the basement. By evening, they were as tired as their parents. All went up to bed at the same time. A few beds still had to be made up, and the oldest ones helped do that.

From that first night in the house, as soon as the family had gone to bed, they would hear the rocking chair sigh and squeak as it rocked in its corner downstairs. It always happened just as soon as the lights were out and each family member was cozily settled in bed.

Whenever anyone jumped out of bed and ran downstairs to see what was happening, the chair was still; the rocking had stopped. The children joked about it, wishing their stairway had a banister, so they could slide down fast and check on the chair.

What made the chair rock remained a mystery. Later the mother had a strange experience in the same house. She was coming up from the dimly lighted basement one day when she plainly felt a hand rest on her shoulder. Briefly. Lightly. Almost like a loving, comforting touch. This was rather bewildering, as she was sure

40

her husband was at work in the farthest field and the children were all in school.

She hurried on up the steps. She looked around, but nothing was there. No one else was in the house at the time. At least, no other mortal.

Herman and Maude

BONNIE JORDAHL REMEMBERS the Palace Theater in Luverne, Minnesota, in its early years. "My mother sold tickets there," she said. "My father was a projectionist, and my sister and I ushered. Oh, but that was a long time ago!"

The Palace Theater at Main and Freeman in Luverne is one of the town's buildings that reflects the early years of Luverne and Rock County. Some have been restored and are on the National Register of Historic Places, as is the Palace.

The year this story was written, the pipe organ that was installed in 1926 in the Palace was being repaired. "When the workers are finished," Bonnie said, "we plan to hold recitals in the theater. Maybe we can also have an old-fashioned silent movie, with organ accompaniment. If that works out, we hope to show it in connection with an Open House. It's also possible that the old ballroom in the building will become a museum. If it does, it will be open during the summers."

The idea for musical accompaniment to silent movies reflects the long-ago days in the Palace, about which some ghost stories have circulated.

Among the known facts are these: the beautiful Palace Theater was built in 1915 by Herman Jochims, the local theater manager, at a cost of $50,000. It was opened for use on September 29, 1915.

Four years later, Herman married Maude. Maude played the piano and later the pipe organ to accompany silent movies shown in the theater. From the start, the theater was used for traveling shows, operatic and dramatic productions, and, later, modern movies with sound.

From time to time, in more recent years, when the building has been in use, a story about the presence of a ghost surfaces. People in the audience and ushers in the aisles said they saw the ghost of Herman Jochims. His favorite place seemed to be the balcony; from there he could keep an eye on what went on and how his theater was being used, and he could be close to Maude, who, it is said, returns to her old place at the organ in the orchestra pit.

Perhaps the couple, by their ghostly presence, hope to keep control over what happens there. It could be that Herman and Maude are responsible for objects being moved or broken or lost. Imagine how an actor felt when the prop he was to pick up from a coffee table at the beginning of Act III was simply not there. Yet it had been there at dress rehearsal the night before and every rehearsal before that!

Herman probably likes to sit in the balcony and listen to his Maude play the organ. When the theater was under repair, no musical accompaniment was planned for any production. But Maude still somehow provided music every now and then.

"Maude may have had a hard time making the break," one Luverne resident offered. "She was so used to sitting there. When she accompanied the old movies, she played beautifully. Now there's usually no one in the pit area, especially in the middle of the night. But folks claim they can still hear the music. Mostly those who leave late at night after a practice. And the janitors, too, when they check the building after everyone else is gone."

One night custodian said, "It was classical music. I've heard it more than once. And it's weird to hear it at midnight when you're turning out the lights and you know you're the last one in the building. One night it was like someone was there turning out the lights ahead of me.

"No one ever hangs around here long, and neither do I. I check all the rooms and finish locking up, and I get out of here as fast as I can. In fact, if you have any questions, save them. I'm out of here!"

That's Enough Now

SUE SAID THAT HER FAMILY LIVED in nine different houses while she was growing up. They moved often because her father worked for lumber companies. When he had a business up and running well, the officials sent him on to another location to set up another business for the company. The family's homes had been located in Iowa, South Dakota, and Minnesota.

"We felt comfortable in some of those houses," Sue said, "where nothing unusual happened. But in others, we were often uneasy because of unexplainable occurrences. I was pretty young then, but I remember one house that you couldn't pay me to enter again now!"

In 1967 Sue's family moved into a house on Smith Avenue in Worthington, Minnesota. At that time, the family consisted of her father, whose first name was Engelbert; her mother, Lorraine; her brother, Kent; Sue; and her married sister Linda, whose husband was serving in Vietnam.

At first, the frame house on Smith Avenue had white wood siding. Later, shakes were installed on the exterior. With its dormer windows and slanting ceilings, it resembled a Cape Cod style house.

Sue said, "The first indication of something different while we lived there was the disappearance of fairly small items such as watches, scissors, and checkbooks. When something was missing, several of us would look for the item, but without success. Invariably, in the next day or so, the missing item would appear again, almost always where it belonged, but sometimes elsewhere, such as on

45

the floor in the middle of the room. This happened more often in winter—or at least we noticed it more then. Maybe it was just that we were in the house more."

The family had a comfortable wooden rocking chair that had a short back, wide arms, and a seat cushion Sue's mother had made for it. Sometimes, when members of the family came home, the chair would be rocking as if someone had just gotten out of it.

Sue said, "It became almost a joke when we came home and found the chair rocking. You know—when you aren't sure about ghosts or about what's going on, you might say, 'Wow! We must have a ghost in the house!' My brother and sister and I would try to make the chair rock by pounding or jumping on the floor near it or by running in and out the door, but it never worked. Then Dad would say, 'There's a reason why the chair is rocking. We just haven't figured it out.'

"We lived in that house from 1967 until the year Dad died. That was in 1994. In the early 1970s, there was a time when we thought we had a thirsty ghost. The folks kept a bottle of liquor tucked into their bedroom wardrobe behind pillows and blankets. They said they kept it handy in case they needed it for medicinal purposes. Sometimes the bottle showed up in plain sight in front of the stacks of bedding. Later on, the bottle was kept in the kitchen and hidden behind the cereal boxes. Sometimes, when the folks came home from work, they found the bottle on the kitchen counter, whether anyone had been in the house or not—at least, anyone who belonged there. And Dad and Mom were always very good about locking the house up whenever they left, so it didn't seem that someone had just walked in while they were gone. The strangest thing about this was that there was never any booze missing. The level of the contents never varied.

"Then in the mid-1970s (by then I was married and had two children), Mom would sometimes surprise me with a phone call. She would say, 'Sue, it's all right if you come over when I'm not here, but I wish you'd have the kids pick up the toys and put them away before they leave.' I hadn't been over there, and neither had the kids.

"We all knew the toys were kept in a box on the stairway to the second floor. Every now and then, when Mom arrived home from work, she would find them scattered on the living room and dining room floors. That was when she would call me. I could hardly blame her. I did go over there sometimes because their house was air conditioned and ours wasn't. But I began to wonder if they had one ghost or two, and one was a child that liked to play with the old toys. Most of the time, though, I thought of the ghost as a man. We always referred to it as 'he.'"

There was another way that the house lent itself to haunting. On the second floor, storage spaces had been built into the outer parts of the rooms, where the slanted ceilings came down toward the floor. One of them was in the hallway visible when one walked up the stairs. The other two storage spaces were in one of the bedrooms. They were large spaces . . . in fact, Sue said she had slept on a bunk bed in one of them—the one with a light in it— when she was fifteen.

The storage spaces had doors with latches that held tight, as one protruding part clicked into the other part when you shut the door. But at various times, the doors would be found open. "When that happened," Sue recalled, "either Mom or Dad would ask us what we were doing in the storage closets, and why we didn't see to it that they were closed when we came out. Mother always liked to keep things neat in the house, so she didn't like it when she looked up the steps and saw all those boxes in the closet.

"This sometimes happened several times a week, but then it didn't happen again for a couple of months. Dad would try to figure out why. He'd check the latches and the storage spaces, but he never found any trace of anyone having opened the closets. Even when I slept in one, the door never opened while I was in there. We never saw any of those doors pop open. That made us think the ghost was a bit antisocial because no tricks were pulled while anyone was there.

"When Dad was ill, it bothered me to find the doors open while Dad was in the house."

About a year after Sue's father died, a realtor (Steve) agreed to try to sell the house. Sue knew he was planning to hold an Open House, but she didn't realize it would be so soon. She was a teacher. Steve and Sue happened to meet in the hall at her school one day, and that's when he told her of the planned Open House that very weekend.

Sue did want to get the house sold as soon as possible in order to finally close the estate. After school on Friday afternoon, she took all her cleaning products and the vacuum over and started in on what seemed an endless task. She wanted to make the house fresh and sparkly, and she worked hard and steadily to do that. She used Carpet Fresh and Windex. She used Pledge on all the woodwork. She dusted, scrubbed, and vacuumed. In fact, she had just turned off the Kirby at about 10:30 that night when she realized how tired she was. She said, "I sat down on the carpet in the middle of the room, exhausted. I cried. I guess I was not only tired, but I was feeling sorry for myself, too.

"All of a sudden, I felt a presence near me in the room, as if someone was trying to comfort me. At the same time, the kitchen light and all the basement lights went off. I couldn't figure out why. The vacuum was already off, so it wasn't affected. It really frightened me. Later, I realized that a fuse had blown just then.

"As I sat there, panicking, it seemed that someone said, 'That's enough now. You've done enough for today.' I can't say now whether it was just a thought I had, or whether it was a voice I heard, but it was as if Dad was saying what he had often said, 'That's enough. We did enough for today.'"

Sue said that since then, at various times, she has felt her father put his hand on her shoulder as if to reassure her that things would be okay.

The only other incident Sue recalled from the past years was one that frightened one of the family severely. She said, "After Mom died in February of 1982, Linda and her family came back just one time, about three months after the funeral. They didn't stay long, and she didn't come back for a whole year and a half. We couldn't figure out why she stayed away so long.

"Later on, when she was home for Dad's funeral, Linda finally explained what had happened that caused her and her family to leave so suddenly that time and not return for so long. She said that, three months after Mom died, she was standing in the upstairs hallway when she felt a cold, icy hand grab her by the shoulder. It scared her so much that she hurried her family out of there immediately, without telling the rest of them why. Originally, they had planned to stay for the weekend."

Sue shuddered visibly when she said, "That was the most frightening incident of all, in the house on Smith Avenue."

Tuned In

SOME EVENTS IN LIFE SEEM TO DEFY logical explanation. The events themselves are interesting and catch our attention, leading to intriguing questions and speculations. We find ourselves trying to figure out the connections.

Are some individuals endowed with special powers? Do they have such a keen awareness that they can perceive danger to loved ones, even at a distance, at the very moment it appears? Is it possible to be "tuned in" somehow to what will happen? Could a person hear the ticking of a clock (when there is no clock around) and know it foretells the ticking away of life's moments? The experiences of a family in one of the border counties of southwest Minnesota suggest this might be true.

Berniece was the person who seemed to be "tuned in," and at a young age. When Berniece was thirteen, she sat by her father's bedside as he lay dying of cancer. She had been told he would not recover, and she spent as much time with him as she could. "I wanted to be with him every moment," she said later. "I loved him very much."

Berniece recalled, "For his last two days, he was incoherent. But when he did open his eyes now and then, I felt that he saw me or Mom or whoever was there. One day in the dead quiet of his room, I heard a ticking sound coming from a corner. His old alarm clock wasn't on the dresser any more, almost as if no one wanted to remind him of time passing. Yet I heard the ticking. I was mystified. I had heard of the insect called the death-watch beetle, a small European wood-borer. It makes a ticking sound thought to be an omen of death. I kept wondering about that ticking sound.

"I was soon aware that each person who came into the room also heard it. It was as though there was an invisible clock in the room, and it seemed to all of us that it was marking off Dad's last moments.

"At the instant of his death, I was sitting next to him, still holding his hand. Dad opened his eyes and looked at me. Then he was gone. At the same time that I heard what Mom called the death rattle, the ticking stopped.

"I don't know if the ticking signaled Dad's approaching death. Some of the relatives thought it was a spiritualistic experience. Others felt it was more like a death rap, a sign."

Berniece told of another incident. Her husband, Jim, was born and grew up in southwest Minnesota. When he was a young boy, the area had few doctors. It was difficult to get one to make a house call from the larger towns like the county seats, especially at night and during a winter storm.

"One stormy night," Berniece said, "Jim's brother, who was seven, suddenly became ill. Later, his family realized he'd had an attack of appendicitis. Complications set in, and the boy died in his mother's arms before morning.

"That night the front door opened, though none of them had opened it. They were sure it had been locked toward evening. There was no reason to unlock it because the doctor couldn't get there, and no one else was expected. They felt it was a sign, but they never really understood it. Neither did they understand why the old violin, stored in its case in the attic, began to play tune after tune."

Berniece described another day thirty years ago. She remembers it clearly, just as if she were watching a movie on tape. She said, "I was standing at the kitchen sink, scrubbing some new garden potatoes to cook for supper. Suddenly I heard my daughter scream out, 'Mommy!'"

Thirteen-year-old Linda, however, was spending a few days with her cousins on their farm about ten miles away. Still, Berniece searched for her. "I was so taken by the realness of her scream that I hunted all through our big three-story house, calling out her name and expecting an answer. None came. I even went outside and walked all the way around the house and yard, listening for her and wondering if she could have come home without my knowing it. She was nowhere in sight.

"I became more scared as the minutes passed. Something seemed to be telling me that she had been hurt or maybe even killed, and I had a strange feeling that her spirit had come to warn me. I tried to shrug off the thought and get on with the day.

"About an hour later, I went shopping for groceries. I couldn't decide which brand of cereal to buy. I didn't really have my mind on what I was doing. But I was trying to be objective and not be persuaded by what came free in the package. That's when the manager came over to me. He said, 'Bernie, someone's here to see you. Come this way with me, please.'

"My thoughts raced to the scream I'd heard. Something had happened to Linnie. I was sure, now. And there, at the front entrance, stood my distraught sister-in-law. She said, 'I have Linnie in the car. You might want to take her to the doctor for stitches. She has a nasty cut on her head.'

"As we hurried to her car, she told me what had happened. 'Linda and Jason were taking lunch out to the field to Mike. He was working less than half a mile from the house, but the kids got thrown off the horse.'

"I asked her how long ago. She said, 'At 11:30.' And that was the exact same time I'd heard Linda scream out, 'Mommy!'"

Now Be at Peace

JULIE'S GRANDFATHER HAD ALWAYS BEEN a major personality in her life. The bond between them strengthened after Julie's father left her mother with the two young sisters, Julie and Linda. That was when Grandpa took his daughter, Carole, and her girls "under his wing," so to speak.

The three moved into the big house where he lived in Minneapolis. Rather than having Carole look for work to support herself and the girls, who were five or six years old at the time, he gave her an allowance so that she could stay home with her daughters. Julie remembers that he treated them to candy and other things they liked, and he took them to the parks, the state capitol, the zoo, and other places they enjoyed.

Grandpa felt it was only natural to help them pass the time in their younger years through activities so enjoyable to them . . . even educational . . . and he was happy to do it. It did seem to alienate other cousins, though, who felt that Julie and Linda were becoming grandfather's favorites.

This story is about Julie, who grew up and eventually married. Even after her marriage, she continued to feel close to her grandfather, while the rift between him and other members of the family continued to widen. When they knew he was taking medication to combat the beginning stages of Alzheimer's, they pointed out that he was doing weird things. For example, late one night, rather than using the bathroom, he urinated in Aunt J's backyard.

53

Later, when Aunt J's daughter was to be married, Grandpa was not invited to the wedding. It could be that those who made up the guest list were only concerned with his health and well-being, but Julie and her mother wondered if Aunt J was afraid she would be embarrassed by his presence or by his actions.

The wedding was to take place in Minneapolis, so when Julie and her husband made the trip there, they stayed at her grandpa's house. For Julie, that was as natural as for daylight to follow dawn. While they were there, they took Grandpa out to dinner one evening. When they returned, Julie and Grandpa walked toward the house while Julie's husband parked the car in front of the garage. That was when Grandpa stumbled on the porch steps. Though Julie tried to keep him from falling, he was too big for her. He fell and hit the back of his head on a concrete step. The next morning, he couldn't speak. He went into convulsions, then a coma. Three days later, he died.

Julie felt extremely guilty about his death. She thought she should have been able to keep him from falling. Later, she said, "After all, I was right there beside him when he stumbled!"

About five years later, Julie was having trouble in her marriage. One night at home, she was sleeping alone when she awoke to a *whoosh . . . whooshing* sound. At the same time, she felt a cold chill. Though she thought the windows were closed, she checked them. They were all closed. She felt a little frightened at first, but she saw nothing unusual in the room while the light was still on. As she settled down again, she felt the definite presence of her grandfather. He seemed to be there in spirit, comforting her, telling her that things were going to be okay. Though he said nothing to her, Julie felt the communication, "Julie, you were not at fault in the matter of my death. I just want you to be at peace about it."

A few months later, Julie's divorce was final. When she married Rick, her present husband, she told him, "I married you because you remind me of my grandfather."

A Creepy Coincidence

CEMETERIES AGAIN. Some are cheerful places peaceably laid out in the open, warmed by the sun and brightened by colorful, blooming plants or artificial wreaths. Others are creepy and dark, their markers lying helter-skelter in the shadows of many trees and shrubs and overgrown with tangled grass and weeds.

Of the latter type, there was one on a hill outside of St. Peter, Minnesota. It was so thick with vegetation that no caretaker could mow it anymore. The undergrowth seemed determined to crowd out or hide the dead. If this verdant hilltop burial site wasn't called Green Cemetery, it should have been.

A young woman tells of a time as a teen-ager, when she and two friends explored that gloomy place one August day. Because of the fast pace at which the incidents took place, her story is short.

When Kathy and her friends Jill and Shawn reached the top of the hill and took the right turn-off, they all got out of Jill's TransAm to have a look around. Where they could brush aside the long grass and tall goldenrod, they looked for inscriptions on headstones. They were intrigued by the neat inscriptions that began "Here lies . . ." or "In memory of . . ." Not all were readable, however, being too worn by age and weather.

Kathy found herself thinking of an epitaph she had read about in a literature class, perhaps of Robert Louis Stevenson or Shakespeare.

Suddenly Kathy started sneezing and coughing. "Must be allergic to one of these weeds," she said aloud.

Jill, near Kath at the time, started teasing. "KOF! KOF! KOF! Katherine Olivia Fox!" That, of course, was Kathy's full name.

"That's silly. Cough isn't spelled KOF, and you know it! Just because J.C. and S.E. don't spell anything in particular, you're jealous. Maybe they would, if I knew your middle initials!"

"Yeah, but it's yours that sounds out to spell cough."

Ignoring Jill, Kathy stopped to set up a marker that had fallen when she had stumbled over it. Beside a tangled lilac, this stone seemed to have neither name nor dates. Brushing away the mottled late-summer lilac leaves, she turned it over and looked closer. She thought she could just make out initials. She bent closer and traced the chiseled-out grooves with her fingertips. Then she suddenly let out a scream, straightened, and ran for the car. Jill and Shawn, not knowing what was wrong, did the same. They piled into Jill's TransAm and headed back to town, leaving the dead to rest in peace.

Safely home and considerably calmed, Kathy told the others what had upset her. "You'd feel the same if you'd found a tombstone tipped over on its front, just sort of waiting for you, with no dates on it yet. But there were initials, all right! And they were the exact same as mine: K.O.F."

Melissa's Ghost

A FEW YEARS AGO, MELISSA HAD AN EXPERIENCE with what she figured had to be a ghost.

The family had just moved into their house in Worthington shortly before this happened. It was late one February night. Melissa said, "I went to bed as usual that night, but I sure didn't fall asleep as usual. Instead, I found myself staring at the ceiling. I heard all the usual creaks and groans our old house made. I heard the TV on downstairs. David Letterman's voice kept me company, so I knew that someone else was still awake down there. It was probably Mom and Dad.

"Soon David Letterman's voice faded away and the soft glow of the hall light faded to darkness. For some reason, I wasn't comfortable even then, when I should have been able to fall asleep easily in the quiet of the hour. Something was wrong. First, I felt a chill. Then I broke out in a sweat. Even pulling the covers up to my chin didn't make me comfortable.

"My sister Mindy and I shared that room. She was about fourteen then. But she was no help; she was sound asleep through all that happened.

"At first, I was afraid to move, and I felt as though I was paralyzed. Every ordinary sound in the house turned into something else, something threatening. The noise from the furnace when it came on made me think an intruder was sneaking around from room to room downstairs. Even the sounds from outside became foreboding. The wind was suddenly someone murmuring menacingly near the window.

"I convinced myself that someone, perhaps a stranger, was present in addition to myself and my three sisters, all of them asleep in our two upstairs bedrooms.

"Finally, in a weak voice, I asked, 'Who's there?' but I doubted if anyone could have heard me. Then I wondered if Mom or Dad could hear me if I screamed. As if I could have screamed!

"I mustered up enough courage to roll off of my waterbed and slip around the corner into the other bedroom where Molly and Sarah slept. I climbed up into the top bunk where Molly, a fifth-grader then, was sound asleep. I made as much commotion as possible climbing up there and flopping down. I hoped it would wake Molly so she could comfort or reassure me. She went right on sleeping. I finally pushed her over and lay down. Sarah, even younger than Molly, was sleeping in the lower bunk. She didn't stir, either.

"Hoping to get back to sleep, I kept my eyes shut tight. But when I heard the stairs creak, my eyes popped open and focused on a figure in the doorway of the room I had just left. As I looked again, looking downward from where I was in Molly's bed, what I saw was the somewhat glowing figure of a young, blonde girl in a light blue dress, seated on the floor, partly in the bedroom and partly in the hall. She was staring into the darkness, toward Mindy's bed. Mindy slept on.

"We always kept our bedroom doors open. The moonlight coming through the windows was just enough to see things in those rooms that night. At first, I thought I was seeing my own reflection in the mirror on the table. To check that out, I moved around a bit, but the figure didn't move. I closed my eyes tightly, thinking the mysterious shape would disappear. But when I looked again, she was still there, not appearing to be menacing or threatening, but just there. Her face was whitish, very clear, and smooth like a little girl's would be. I wasn't scared enough to scream or to get out of there, or maybe I was too scared to do either.

"Finally, somehow, even all stressed out from fear and uncertainty and trying my best to figure out what was happening, I drifted off to sleep.

"Afterward, the only thing I ever found out that might have had some connection was that a woman was once found dead in our bathroom, before we moved in."

Recently, Molly found out a little more. She talked with Mabel, their neighbor lady, hoping to find some explanation or reason for the ghostly figure. Mabel said she had grown up with Pauline, the woman who used to live in the house. She had a son, also living there. When she was about eighty, Pauline took sick.

Mabel had often run over to see Pauline, and when she found out she was sick, Mabel took her a bowl of warm chicken noodle soup. It was on a Sunday, when Pauline's son was home. He answered Mabel's knock. Mabel said, "I missed Pauline in church this morning, and I just wanted to know if she's all right."

He didn't invite Mabel in, but he accepted the bowl of soup and said, "I'll take it in to her."

On Monday, Pauline's niece Bette came to Mabel's home. She asked, "Have you seen Aunt Pauline lately?" They talked about the situation and decided to check on Pauline to make sure she was all right. In fact, Bette asked her husband, who had a key to the house, to come along. They went over, unlocked the door, and called out to rouse Pauline if she was resting. When they didn't get a response, they searched the house and found Pauline on the bathroom floor. Her head had been split open somehow, and there was a lot of dark, dried blood. Pauline was dead. Looking around a little more, they found her purse, but it had been emptied of any money she might have had in it.

The authorities didn't solve the case and could declare it an accident or something else. They weren't sure. Maybe Pauline had fallen and hit her head on the bathtub. Maybe it was murder, with robbery the motive. Maybe she had died a natural death.

Molly and her sisters never did figure out whose spirit Melissa saw that one February night. Melissa said it was the figure of a young girl, but she couldn't see how that connected with the elderly woman's death. Was there another person, younger and deeply affected by that death, one who missed Pauline very much and came in spirit to look for her? Had Pauline lived in the house as a young girl, and was it her spirit who had returned?

At the time of this writing, Melissa is in her twenties. She still believes she saw a ghost that night. And, to this day, she says that whenever she's upstairs in that house, she feels sort of a chill. She also looks ahead of and behind herself as she walks into one of those bedrooms. And whenever she walks into the bathroom, she pulls the shower curtain aside and looks behind it, just in case.

Molly admits, "I always feel scared in that room to this day, ever since I saw that ghost that night."

Up in Smoke

ISABEL'S FATHER FREQUENTLY TALKED about this happening that took place somewhere near Cottonwood in Lyon County.

He was one of eleven children. At the time, nine were living, along with their parents. Isabel's father was third from the oldest and was thirteen or fourteen years old at the time the incidents climaxed and ended, so he remembered them clearly.

Every one of the nine children and both parents saw an apparition. Not just everyone at one time, but different members of the family and at different times. Over the years, the shape of a rather smallish woman, always dressed in black, appeared to them. She never talked. She never touched or harmed anyone. She always appeared upstairs. She would go in and out of the bedrooms and hall, seeming to be walking but also seeming to go through the walls. At no time did they see her open doors.

When the mysterious woman last appeared in 1917 or 1918, there had just been a fire. The house burned down to the ground, and the whole family—all nine children and their parents—stood looking forlornly at the total destruction.

Other people had come to watch the house burn down. Friends and neighbors came and stayed awhile, staring at the leaping flames and awkwardly trying to express shock or sympathy. Some offered to help, but there was nothing to do. Finally all left the scene except the family. They stood huddled closely together, looking

61

toward the ashes and embers, all that remained of their home. They stood mesmerized, not yet fully realizing their situation. They stood in shock, immobile, quiescent.

And as they stood and watched, they all saw the same familiar woman figure walk across those hot coals. This time she was dressed in glorious white and untouched by the flames. They watched her rise and disappear like a puff of air in the wall of smoke that still lingered over the ruins.

Deadman's Hill

ACROSS THE LINE FENCE ON DEADMAN'S HILL north of Willmar, Minnesota, stood an old, weather-beaten house. The rock walls of the cellar had caved in on one side, so the house hung at an angle. A lilac bush growing beside the front door had slid into the cellar, roots and all, after the wall gave way. The lilac continued to grow and bloom each year, though it was hidden from all except the children whose curiosity led them to the cave-in, especially when they noticed the deep lavender color or the fragrance of the flowers when almost everything else was still fairly drab in early spring.

Alice and her brother had to go over the hill to take the cows to and from the back pasture, so they went through the old farmyard many times. They knew the lilac grew down in the hole. And they soon began to realize that the basement lilac wasn't the only odd thing on the hill. They suspected someone or something lingered there. It gave them an uncanny feeling whenever they heard the stories others told.

During the early years of World War II, the neighbor whose grandfather had bought the land that included that farmsite on the hill decided to tear down what was left of the old buildings. His intent was to build a henhouse and a shed, using the old lumber. He would also have more land to use as pasture for his beef cattle, once the old buildings were gone. It seemed like a good arrangement to him, and he went ahead with the plan.

After the old house was torn down, the workmen pushed the foundation in on top of the struggling lilac bush and filled the hole. They didn't want the cattle falling into the cellar and getting hurt.

The henhouse went up. Not too long afterward, the farmer's daughter claimed to have seen a ghost when she went into the new henhouse to gather the eggs. No one paid much attention to her at first, because she was at an age when a vivid imagination was not unusual.

Not much later, the farmer's wife and one of his sons also claimed they saw ghosts, or whatever they were, in the henhouse. They insisted that as soon as they were inside and the door was closed so the hens couldn't escape, they felt as though someone else was also in there, though they could never see anyone else. From then on, the building stood empty. No one wanted to enter it, because of what they had heard. They began to wonder if the ghosts had survived because the old lumber had been used for the new building on Deadman's Hill.

In 1938, Alice's father still farmed with horses. He decided to plow the pasture, including the hill. He tried all three teams on the plow at different times. The horses would buck and act crazy every time he got near the hill. It was as if something spooked them, although he saw nothing unusual.

Finallly he gave up on the horses. He borrowed a neighbor's Fordson tractor to finish plowing and working up the field.

When April came, he tried to use the horses again, this time to drill grain. The teams bucked. They refused to go up the hill. He had to seed that hill with a Cyclone seeder, by hand.

Alice remembers him saying at the time, "Animals can sense dangers that people can't. There has to be something on that hill."

After that, Alice's father didn't try to plant a crop on the hill until they were able to use all tractor machinery. Even then, he never let anyone go near the hill in late afternoon.

The family began to notice that the horses weren't the only animals with that special sense. During a drought one summer, the pasture was getting very dry and brown, but for some unexplainable reason, the hill was still green. As hungry as they were, the cattle refused to feed on the lush green grasses of the hill.

The same family had a good collie watchdog named Rover. Even Rover was wary. Sometimes he would follow the others up the hill. At other times, he would whine at the bottom of the hill until they went back down to him. Rover's reactions to whatever was on that hill made the children a little more careful, and a little more scared, even though they weren't sure what frightened them.

The Ghosts of Loon Lake Cemetery

SOME OF THE OLD, ABANDONED CEMETERIES in the Midwest hold their stories close. Fenced, hidden under tangled weeds and brush or covered by an accumulation of leathery oak leaves, some tombstones speak of Civil War veterans come home for burial. Others tell of infants who lived for only days or weeks. Still others name several children of the same family, or children and parents, who died within the same year, probably during an epidemic. Some markers are inscribed with loving messages, some with solemn warnings for the living.

Jackson County has a cemetery called Loon Lake Cemetery that lies south of Lakefield not far from the Minnesota State Highway 86 between Petersburg and Sioux Valley. The last known burial there was in 1926. Somehow, ghost and witch stories have become associated with that burial ground, and the legend has grown and changed over the years.

The surrounding area boasts a golf course and Loon Lake Grocery Store. The cemetery can be reached either over dry land or by a treacherous, swampy route that has mired newspaper staff writers.

This burial place has had its share of visitors, considering that it's abandoned. Relatives of the dead came, the family of Horace Alexander Dickinson, who was the father of Lillian Jones of Reading. In October 1987 Jones told Carrie Sword, a *Worthington Daily Globe* staff writer at the time, that her family used to make visiting the cemetery an all-day outing. They would go by horse and buggy up to the cemetery to "tend the graves and the grounds."

There is no longer a road up the pine-covered hill to the graves, but Jones remembers Loon Lake Cemetery as a childhood place. And she remembers that her grandmother, Mary Jane Dickinson, is buried there.

It could be that the ghost stories and the legend of a witch's curse began with the same Mary Jane, who, according to Jones, had some unusual powers, but she was also a "Christian woman who cared for her ten children and kept her family together," according to Sword's article. Lillian Jones said her grandmother was not a witch, but the legend could have developed because Mary Jane did have extra-sensory perception.

Other visitors to the cemetery since Jones went there with her family have not tended the graves. In fact, there have been frequent beer parties there through the years. Perhaps those gatherings generated the story that as many as three witches are buried there.

The legend rules that anyone who walks there will die an unnatural death. One of the alleged three witches, also named Mary Jane, supposedly died when the people of nearby Petersburg, east of Loon Lake Cemetery, cut off her head with an ax shortly before Halloween in 1881. That Mary Jane was not the grandmother of Lillian Jones.

Part of the legend of the burial place is that if one jumps over the grave of one of the witches three times, that person will die. Another detail is that the witches' curse will descend on anyone who misbehaves through rowdiness or vandalism near their graves.

If the cemetery is haunted, the ghosts could be any of a number of people interred there but still wandering in the vicinity, as spirits, for one reason or another. One of the Mary Janes might be trying to prove her special powers that people ascribe to her. Or the four infants buried there might be looking for their parents, Mr. and Mrs. A. Foshage. Or "J.Pete" isn't happy with the condition of his tombstone, lying in bits in the long grass and weeds, so that visitors can't even pronounce his full name. If he was a pioneer settler, he deserves proper identification. Willie Brown, whose marker bears only his name and the date 1910, could be wanting the rest of his story told. Or Clarinda Allen, who died shortly before Halloween in 1885, might be looking for her relatives.

It is said that when John Dickinson died on October 13, 1877, at the age of twelve years, nine months, and twenty-two days, he was the first person buried in Loon Lake Cemetery. That was when Sylvanus Dickinson gave some land to the settlers of Loon Lake. The next spring they moved the bodies of their dead from their homestead burial sites to the cemetery where John Dickinson's body had been buried the previous fall.

That was in the early years, when at least sixty-seven tombstones were upright and a spirit of loving care surrounded them. But now, over one hundred years later, the atmosphere is very different. There are ghost stories and the legend of the witches' curse. Considerable damage has been done by vandals. According to Jones, only eighteen stones are still recognizable.

Perhaps one Mary Jane's tombstone is in the bottom of the lake. Perhaps her ghost haunts the cemetery and the lake, looking for her marker and wanting it rightfully placed. That could, possibly, put an end to the legend and to the apprehension people feel about the cemetery.

Some Ghosts Bring Peace

EDNA AND HERMAN BOUGHT A HOUSE even though the neighbors told them it was haunted. It shouldn't have been any surprise to them when "things" started happening. These were little things, at first, as on one night after all the family had retired to their rooms, ready for a night's sleep—some in second floor bedrooms, the youngest in a first-floor bedroom, and one on the davenport. The one on the davenport saw a shape going down the hall. Edna and Herman heard a noise as if someone had walked out the door. All the family heard it, wherever they were bedded down. The parents checked this out but found no one missing.

When Edna's mother died, a neighbor "sat the house" the day of the funeral. As the volunteer dozed in a rocking chair, she suddenly woke up to find Edna's mother in the room. She was wearing a blue-flowered dress and a gold brooch—the same dress and brooch she wore laid out in her casket.

The ghost spoke to the surprised house-sitter. She said, "I wanted to see how much remodeling Herman had got done—wanted to see how it was coming along, before I leave. But I'd better go now, or I'll be late for my own funeral." This happened about two hours before the service, while the family was out having lunch.

After Edna's husband, Herman, died, Edna and their youngest daughter could hear music coming from a corner of the living room. Several times, one of them got up to make sure the radio or TV hadn't been left on with the volume low. They were always both off. The

69

music was all Irish and Scottish, played softly until late hours, as if the absent loved one wanted them to relax, now that the difficult time was over. Friends and neighbors who stopped in also heard the music, and it was very relaxing for all. Sometimes the family and guests also heard voices coming from above the ceiling, near a fireplace in one corner of the living room.

Some time later, Edna remarried. The couple occupied the same house. One night when the two were playing cards at the kitchen table, they both saw Herman come from a back room into the front of the house and go out the front door. It had to be Herman's ghost, Edna thought. Who else? But what a strange situation!

Another time, at dusk, Edna and her second husband were playing cards when Edna excused herself to go to the bathroom. On her way back, she saw something or someone floating up and around the plants in the living room against the window. Then the shape disappeared. It seemed to rise toward the ceiling; then it was gone. Edna sensed a calmness rather than fear at this occurrence. She wondered if she had just seen the spirit of her mother. When Edna went back to the card game, her partner took one look at her and said, "You saw something! I can tell by the look on your face. Was it another ghost?"

Edna told him what she had seen and also about the time a month or so earlier when she couldn't sleep and had gone down to the loveseat in the living room with a cup of warm milk, trying to lure sleep. It was close to midnight when she saw something moving outside the window. It was a shape hovering above the flowerbed. She moved closer to look out. The shape spoke to her through the window, "I'm an angel. I came down here with your mother. She wants to see your flowers. She always loved them so. But don't let her see you. She doesn't want to frighten you."

Edna backed up from the window and watched from there. She saw one shape moving out by the road and another by the flowerbed. "Then they both moved away," she said, "leaving me feeling very peaceful.

"After that," Edna continued, "we got out the Ouija Board. We asked it, 'Was that a ghost?' It went to NO. 'What was it, then?' It spelled out the word SPIRIT. We hadn't thought of that. 'My mother's?' I asked. And the board went right to YES."

A son-in-law of Edna's died of cancer at age thirty-nine, just a few years before this story was told. One night Edna and her husband were sitting in the living room. Suddenly the room turned cold. They couldn't figure it out. After all, it was July! They reached for the afghans and were more comfortable. One of them checked the other rooms, and they were all as warm as one would expect.

After they went to bed that night, Edna started thinking about what had happened. She got up and went out to the living room. She sat down on the loveseat in the dark room. It was still cold there.

Edna asked, "What?"

A strong scent of roses in bloom pervaded the room while a voice like that of her son-in-law said, "There's going to be an accident."

Edna didn't want to hear that message. She went to bed and covered her ears. But that didn't end it. She was frightened now. She kept thinking about the cold room and the roses and the message.

A little later that same July, six or seven friends sat around the kitchen table playing cards. Edna felt the cold and smelled the roses. Then she heard the same voice as before, with the same message: "Be careful, Mother. There's going to be an accident. It could be you."

In the next little while, Edna left for work, a night shift. "On the way," she said, "I tried to stay calm and be careful. But I looked up to see an on-coming semi. A car was trying to pass the semi and coming right at me. I knew we would crash head-on. The feeling of cold and the fragrance of roses filled the car."

The next Edna knew, she found herself stopped on the shoulder, just as the on-coming car went by. She was okay. She explained, "I believe the ghost had protected me. Saved me."

Edna and her husband and a grandson who spent a lot of time at their house puzzled about the strange noises they heard, like little crashes. Edna finally called a pastor and told him about the things that had been happening. He told Edna, "Someone died in or near the house several years ago. I know that, but I don't know how he died."

Edna wonders if some of the sounds and forms were the manifestations of the spirit of the person who died—not wanting to leave, not ready to make the break, or having some unfinished business.

Fairly recently, the couple and their grandson heard footsteps going upstairs and crossing the hall into the big room, where the bed was always made up. Several times they found the covers pulled back on that bed and the pillow dented as if someone had slept there. This was so upsetting that Edna, who had usually felt calm and at peace with the ghosts of the house, actually called the police to check the bed before the covers were once more pulled up over the pillow.

Neither these strange occurrences nor the actions of the huge tree behind the house drove the family away. "That tree," Edna told me, "has a life of its own. Like a cat with nine lives. At one time that old tree had four large trunks, like four trees in one. In 1972, one trunk fell on our two cars. In 1974, one trunk fell across the dining room and caved in the roof during a storm. In August of 1976, a tornado hit Heron Lake. Every light in town went out. The largest trunk of the tree, the only one remaining, crashed against the back of our house, causing extensive damage, but it was almost as if the tree was holding our house so the tornado couldn't blow it away. Like giant arms, the branches reached across to each side and over the top of the house, securing it, though damaging it, too."

Edna thinks that perhaps the tree has been more than a tree. Perhaps its four trunks, now diminished to one huge, tall, roughly shaped stub of a trunk, figured more in the history of the house and its spirits than anyone will ever know. But several years after Edna gave me her story, she learned more about the Heron Lake house where these ghostly experiences had taken place.

Edna said the new information came to her when a gentleman and two ladies came to talk with her. She said, "They all had the same uncle and aunt, who lived just two houses from ours. They had witnessed strange goings-on in their youth. In their visit with me as adults they recalled those incidents and related them to me."

They told Edna that a family by the name of Greier used to live in the Heron Lake house. Ed Greier, his wife, Lilah, and her mentally handicapped daughter, Mattie, once lived there together.

As a young girl, Lilah had lived somewhere in the South. No one remembered what state. One year she made a trip back down there and brought back a black girl in her middle teens to help her and to be a nanny to Mattie. She called the black girl Zoie, and she pronounced it Zo-ee.

In the back yard of the Greier home several large trees provided welcome shade, and a border of lilac bushes walled the yard off somewhat from the street. But when Zoie and Mattie were out in the yard, they could sometimes be seen by others through breaks in the line of lilacs. Mattie was often seen pushing a doll buggy. Sometimes she appeared between the bushes and frightened others, such as these two ladies when they were girls and visiting their aunt and uncle. They were probably frightened because they were young and didn't understand Mattie's problems and personality.

The two young girls had heard their parents and their aunt and uncle discussing the things that happened at that house—things they all thought were strange.

Apparently the black girl had a boyfriend in the South. Eventually he worked his way north to Minnesota and found Heron Lake and his girlfriend.

The young man was not allowed in the house, but Mr. Greier let him stay in the small red barn that stood off to one side, behind the house. This barn once served as a stable for the Greiers' horses used in cart racing and for riding.

The talk in the neighborhood was that Mrs. Greier was afraid that the young black man might talk Zoie into going back down south with him.

One day the young man failed to come out of the little red barn anymore. When Mr. Greier went to check on him, he found him strung up with a rope from the rafters. Although everyone who heard this shocking news expressed an opinion, no one really knew the facts—except, or course, the one who was responsible. There were some folks in the area who eventually thought it was the ghost of the young black man who was heard walking on the staircase and in the upper bedrooms of the house. If it's true that ghosts are sometimes the result of a violent or unpleasant death, this could well be true.

At any rate, Edna says, "To this day, the case of the young black man's death was never solved. Most people of the time and place have forgotten about it. Many new residents have never heard the story. Only the few oldsters in and around Heron Lake still remember."

Steps to the Music

SOUNDS PLAY A PART IN MANY GHOST STORIES. Some people hear music from unidentifiable sources. Others hear footsteps.

As a young woman, Orene lived on a farm near Storden in Cottonwood County. She recalls hearing someone walking up and down the stairs to the second floor. One time when she heard the footsteps, she opened the door at the bottom of the staircase. She could follow the sound on its way up, but she didn't catch sight of the ghost. It seemed to be the case that when members of the family went up or down the stairs to their bedrooms, the other footsteps were never heard. Only when none of the family were using the staircase did they hear the strange sounds.

Orene's younger sister Harriet heard them once and decided to figure it out. She bravely walked up the stairs behind the footsteps. Each time she heard a step, she took another careful one up. And she groped courageously ahead with her arms, but she found no one there and felt nothing in the space ahead of her. She was disappointed, and the reaon for the sounds remained a mystery.

At about the same time, Orene was interested in learning to play the piano. When she first tried it, she could pick out a melody with her right hand in a sort of pick-and-peck way, but she couldn't figure out how to chord. Frustrated, she let her attention stray from the keyboard to the sounds of the footsteps on the stairs. The stairway went up from one corner of the same parlor where she sat at the piano. She listened. The footsteps were there again. She was keyed up, and in her nervous state she opened the door and followed the sounds up the steps. Again, she found nothing there, but when she came down, closed the door, and went back to the piano, she found she could play any song she wished, even though she couldn't read notes. She was playing by ear.

"You should have seen me," she said. "I sat there on the piano stool and lifted my hands and moved my body lightly to the rhythms of the music, like a professional playing for an audience. And I didn't need anyone to turn the page. I just played on and on, from one song to another. It was unbelievable."

An Odd Occurrence

ABOUT THIRTY YEARS AGO, MARGARET had what she called a very strange experience. She said, "It was a gloomy, rainy day. There was nothing special going on, and it wasn't a pleasant enough day to do anything outdoors, so I thought it was a good time to do the laundry.

"I sorted the soiled clothes and linens from the hamper into baskets and carried one load to the laundry room, where I went ahead with it. I put a load of white and light things and some detergent in the washer, and I set the controls for it to do its thing. The washer was on the main floor, so while it was washing the clothes for me, I was doing odds and ends around the house.

"When the washer stopped running through its cycles, I went back to transfer the clean clothes to the dryer right next to it. While everything else was just part of a routine task, suddenly there was this ball of light in front of me, hovering above the dryer. It was a mass of light—greenish—smallish—about the size of a baseball. I had never seen anything like it. It hung there for a bit, suspended over the dryer. Then it sort of jumped up to the porcelain light fixture on the side wall. The green ball itself wasn't distorted in any way, but that light on the wall went out right then, as if some force or power had put it out. I couldn't figure out what was happening."

"I was startled, of course, and I guess a little scared. It had happened so suddenly. And there I was, all alone, with no clue as to what was going on. I could almost feel the hair on the back of my neck stand up. It gave me an uneasy feeling."

Margaret finished the story quickly. "I didn't stick around to try to figure out what I had seen or what was happening. I just got out of there, real fast. And—so far, at least—it hasn't happened again.

"Several years later, though, I noticed an interesting article in a Minneapolis newspaper. It told about green ball lightning. Printed with the article was a request for anyone who had had such an experience to write in about it. I didn't write in, and I never did see anything else about it, but as I reflected on it later, I really wondered what it was all about."

Margaret wasn't easily convinced that her unusual experience could be explained by an informative newspaper article about ball lightning. "Besides," she said, "what I read said that the 'luminous ball' was often blood-red in color. This one wasn't. It was greenish, and I've heard people talk about greenish masses of light when they tell of ghostly experiences. I had probably had enough scary experiences in my lifetime to result in unexplainable phenomena, but I hadn't had anything like this happen before. Just thinking about it still gives me goose bumps."

Death Raps Recognized

LORRAINE'S FIRST EXPERIENCE with a ghost in her family happened when she was only four, when her mother's parents were living with them.

Grandmother was very sick in the hospital in nearby Sioux City on that particular day. Lorraine was at the foot of the stairs in their home in southwest Minnesota when something or someone came sliding down the banister. Lorraine told her mother about it. Her mother looked up and said, "Lorraine, there's no one there. But Grandma's very sick. Maybe it's Grandma—or the spirit of Grandma."

From that moment on, Lorraine's mother stayed close to her daughter as though she knew strange things would happen, and she didn't want her child to be frightened by them.

That night, a wind-up alarm clock fell off the dresser onto the floor. It landed face down and stopped. The time on the clock was at four A.M.—the exact time that the grandmother died. Lorraine remembers hearing the family talk about that.

After that grandmother's death, the family moved to another house. Grandpa stayed with them, and he lived upstairs. He hardly ever got out of bed due to the weakness of old age.

About a year later, another clock fell off the dresser. it was a beautiful porcelain boudoir clock, and it had always been kept beside Lorraine's mother's bed. It landed face down that night, and it stopped at the time of Grandpa's death.

To the family, this seemed more than just a coincidence.

A few years later, when Lorraine was nine, her grandmother on her father's side was in the hospital in Sioux City. That December, the doctors diagnosed her illness as cancer.

At that time, Lorraine's father always left for work by 5:30 A.M. Lorraine's mother got up to get breakfast for him. After he left, she would go back upstairs to bed. One morning, about an hour after her mother had returned to bed, the piano downstairs started playing. It woke the whole family. Lorraine's mother said, "The cat is probably walking on the keys."

Lorraine went downstairs to check. The cat wasn't anywhere to be seen. In fact, the piano keyboard was closed.

Lorraine and her mother went back to bed, but the mother had recognized the incident as another "death rap."

These signals had been following Lorraine's mother all her life. This time, she got in bed with the children so as to be near them until it was time for them to get up for school. About nine o'clock that morning, while the children were in school, the call came at the house. Grandmother (Lorraine's father's mother) had passed away.

When Lorraine was almost twelve and after another move to another house in southwest Minnesota, something else occurred. Aunt Zephrey, Lorraine's mother's aunt, was married to a peace officer in another state. The officer was transporting a prisoner to a facility in a larger city. Somehow the prisoner jumped the sheriff and killed him. A clock stopped again. It was another windup model. It fell off the stand beside Lorraine's mother's bed in the daytime. Later that day, the call came relaying the message that the sheriff had died.

Lorraine said there were eight children in her mother's family: her mother, six aunts, and one uncle to

Lorraine. All but three had died before Lorraine's own mother died at age fifty-nine. Each time one died, there was a signal to Lorraine's mom, so she would know.

When Lorraine's dad's mother died, the piano had played. When her dad's father died, the signal was different. He died after attending a wrestling match. He got in the car to go home and had a heart attack. At the time, those at home were playing cards. Lorraine's mother looked at her husband and said, "There's something wrong." Then, for no apparent reason, the pot of coffee she had gotten up to make fell from her hand. Fifteen minutes later the call came informing the family that Grandpa had died of the heart attack.

Lorraine's parents had been living in their own home when Lorraine's mother died in 1974. After the funeral, Lorraine's father couldn't go into the bedroom his wife had used. Each time he approached the door, he heard the music of heavenly choirs.

Lorraine's mother died in the hospital at about six P.M. That night, she also appeared at the house and talked kindly and gently to her daughter. She asked her daughter not to argue about dividing the belongings, and to let Father live with her and her husband.

About a year and one-half before this story was disclosed, Lorraine's father died. He had lived with Lorraine and her husband in Worthington, according to the last wish of his wife. He never felt quite at ease there, though. And it was through no fault of his daughter's, nor his son-in-law's. He just never wanted the door to his room closed. He wanted to hear their voices and be near the people he loved.

After his death, Lorraine herself wanted the door closed. It was an extra bedroom, and they no longer needed to keep it warm. Lorraine wanted to shut the register and the door and save on the heating costs. But the door wouldn't stay shut, even when it was closed all the way and the latch caught. The thought came to Lorraine then that her father's spirit didn't want to be away from his family.

What a close family! And what a good spirit among them—the gentle announcement each time a death occurred and signs afterwards that the departed still remained among them—in spirit.

A Scrap of Cloth

DEE'S MOTHER WAS BORN IN 1889, a century before this story was first offered. She and her three sisters told their children later that on the farmplace where they lived as girls, something wasn't right.

The farm was in one of the counties near the southern border of Minnesota. A cemetery bordered the farm. This was back in the horse-and-buggy days, when horses were needed for transportation and field work.

But when the horses on that farm were in the barn, they could often be heard stomping and snorting as though fighting something off or fighting among themselves. The girls didn't go very close to the barn when they heard this, but their father did. He would hear the sounds of boards being ripped loose and flying around, hitting the walls and other things inside the barn. He expected more than once to spend time and energy clearing the debris off the feed bunks and the floor. He thought surely all the hay racks would have to be straightened and the feed boxes put up again. But when he went in to check, he found the horses quiet, no boards loose, everything in order.

On another occasion on the same place, the girls' father, the farmer, came up from the barn on a winter day. As he approached the house, he saw that his wife was hanging the washing on the lines. The shirts and overalls were quickly freezing and swaying stiffly in the bitter cold air.

He asked her if supper was ready. She didn't answer, so he figured she was cold and just wanted to finish quickly. He went on into the house, where he found his wife in the kitchen, stirring a pot of steaming stew.

They both looked around outside. They found no one out there, no clothes basket, and no clothes on the line, just a fragment of gray cloth frozen to the line under one clothespin. That made such an impression on the girls that they never forgot it.

In the same house, Dee and her sisters often heard someone walking around upstairs. When they went up to look, there was no one. All was in order.

Later, the parents sold the house to another family who were openly told it was haunted. The new owners also heard the horses stomping in the barn and heard footsteps upstairs in the house. They asked their priest to come over and see what he could do.

The priest came. His decisive action took place outside the house and barn. He walked around in the cemetery next to the fence line. He did whatever a priest does in such a situation and with such a request for help. After he left, the new owners heard no more unexplainable noises.

The original buildings on the farm are all gone now, but the cemetery is still there, just over the half-buried fence.

Katie Thinks She Has a Protector

AFTER KATIE'S GRANDFATHER JACOB passed away in 1971, his house near Grand Rapids was bought and sold a couple of times. A few years after his death, the house burned to the ground. The family thought maybe it was arson.

After Jacob's death, but shortly before the fire, Katie was living with her parents near Grand Rapids. She was nineteen or twenty then. She said, "I had a bedroom in their basement." Then she began to tell about several strange experiences she had there.

"One night, after I went to bed and the room was dark, I turned my head to see someone standing by my bed, looking at me. I sat up and asked 'him' what he was doing there. He disappeared. I say 'he' now, or 'him,' because the apparition looked very much like my deceased grandfather. The rest of that night, I slept in my parents' living room.

"A few nights later, the ghost (if that's what it was) appeared again, this time waking me. When I woke up, I felt his hand on my arm, but I had no feeling from that point of contact on down to my hand, as if there was no circulation there. It was a strange feeling. Again, I asked what he wanted. Again, he just disappeared.

"On one night when he appeared in my bedroom, I could see him outlined as though a bright light shone behind or around his head, similar to the way angels are sometimes shown in contemporary TV movies."

Around that time, Katie was given a cat as a gift. I vaguely recall that she named it Cindy. On one appearance, the apparition walked away from Katie's bed and walked right through the closet door. When Katie turned the light on, she noticed that Cindy was watching the closet door as if she had also seen what Katie had seen.

Reflecting on the strange incidents in that house, Katie said, "There were many nights when I could feel something or someone moving back and forth on the foot of my bed. When I would turn on the light to see what it was, there was never anyone there. None of my family could have been playing tricks on me, because none of them would go down to the basement in the dark. They always said they could run into or stumble over too many things there.

Katie said, "After Grandpa's house burned, there were no visitations for a while. I was puzzled about that."

Katie told about other occurrences involving other members of the family. "One afternoon," she said, "My mother was in the kitchen when she heard something in the basement. It sounded like a pot cover was rolling around in circles on the cement floor. When she went down to see what it was, there was nothing on the floor that would account for the sounds she heard.

"Another thing . . . we have about two dozen slide cartridges from family vacations, reunions, and school projects. Though the slides have been sorted and put in order a number of times, every time they are taken out to be viewed, we find them out of order, upside down, backwards. Since Mom and Dad are the only occupants of the house now, the slides are never touched in their customary place in an upstairs bedroom, unless we take them out to view them, usually at family gatherings. It's uncanny how we often find them out of order!

"One winter night, Mom and I were sitting up watching the late show. Most of the lights were out. Suddenly we both saw something white drift past the window up at the peak end of the house. It made us think of a bed sheet, but—except to look out the window—we didn't investigate until daylight. When we looked outside then, there was nothing lying in the snow. There were no tracks, no marks at all."

Katie said that when family friends stayed with her parents, they would see, feel and hear the same things. Even now, those who visit there hear footsteps upstairs, going from room to room. They hear movement they can't explain. "This is especially unnerving when you're there alone," Katie said.

"I moved into town from my parents' home and moved several times within just a few years. No matter where I lived, I was still visited. Whether I lived in a house or in an apartment, the appearances occurred in each place I lived. They were all in the Grand Rapids area. In each place, I could feel someone walking or moving about somehow on the foot of my bed. In my current home, I sometimes feel like I'm being watched. Out of the corner of my eye, I can see a shape—maybe the shape of a person—but when I turn my head, the shape is gone.

"At first I felt threatened by the apparition. I wondered why I was singled out. But now I think my mother has also seen glimpses of the ghost. Since no one has been harmed by him and since he appeared mostly only to me, I came to consider him my protector. I feel that he has always 'been there' for me. His presence has become quite comforting, so much so that I miss him when I don't 'see' him for a while. I hope I'll be visited again.

"He seems to be around more when there is disruption in my life. Maybe he hasn't been around for a while because I'm happy and content in my current situation."

Saved by the Bell

"WHY NOT? IT'S HALLOWEEN, but what can happen? Do you think there's someone in that old building?"

"Naw. It hasn't been used for years. C'mon! Let's go."

"Okay, but we all stick together, whatever happens. Agreed?"

"Like glue. Even if it's scary, I'll take a challenge any day!"

"Or night?"

"Or night. You bet!" And with Jamie's last remark, the three friends headed for the old schoolhouse.

It was almost midnight, but their parents wouldn't be missing them. All three kids worked at the A&W at the edge of town and had just gotten off work. Jamie and Tom felt safe when they walked past their house on the way toward the center of town. All the lights were off except the porch light. That meant their mom and dad were off in dreamland. Rich lived just beyond the school. He wouldn't be going by his house until after their adventure.

The old brick schoolhouse was just one of the dilapidated buildings in this ghost town, one of several in southwest Minnesota. It hadn't been used as a school since consolidation. It was considered too run down to repair. No one even believed it could be restored, though there had been some talk about that. It was simply a relic of the years when it stood as a symbol in the once-booming town. Now owls spooked the place at night with their "Who-who-hoo-hoo-hoo," and bats flew in and out of the bell tower at regular hours.

The three adventurers went around to the janitor's door at the back. They found it swaying on one hinge. Inside, they faced complete darkness. Rick took out his pocket flashlight. Cardboard barrels either upright or on their sides confronted them, making it hard to get through to the long hall.

Once they reached the hall, they were able to find a first-floor classroom. There they found everything in complete disorder, except for the teacher's desk. It was as neat and organized as if someone were ready for the next day of school. The few remaining students' desks were either turned over and broken or, if standing whole, were cleared of their papers and pencils.

On a shelf at the side of one room, stacks of books waited to be passed out. On the board were lists of names, each with a set of figures, possibly demerit marks, but it was hard to read the chalk writing, with Rich's flashlight flickering dimmer by the minute.

The three decided to find the gym. They did and went in cautiously. The doors slammed behind them.

"No! Now we're in complete dark!"

"What's the matter with your flashlight?"

"Why didn't you bring one?"

They were all shouting at once. They tried to open the doors, but they seemed to have locked automatically when they slammed.

"There has to be an exit. You have to be able to get out of a gym," Tom said, a little too loudly it seemed to the others. He and Jamie started down one wall, feeling their way to the corner and the adjacent wall while Rich did the same, going the other direction.

Before long Tom's voice broke through the darkness. "Here! I found it! Here's the other door. I knew there had to be one near the bleachers!"

They all pushed on the door until it creaked open far enough for them to get out into the hall again. Then they took the short stairway down to the boiler room. There, a little light came in through the dirty window.

"Must be from the street light at the back alley," Rich mused.

"Good!" Jamie said. "I'll take every bit of light I can get. It's too spooky in here!"

"Hey, Jamie, girl or not, don't go chicken on us. We're all in this together, and we stick together to the end. Remember?"

"All right. But it's still spooky. What now?" And they moved toward a door that hung open and found themselves out in a hall.

Suddenly they heard noises, like a door opening and closing down the hall. Then they heard muted voices, as of a teacher giving instructions in low tones or maybe children reciting and singing. Their own hearts pounded. Their breathing became fast and shallow as they tried to stay quiet. Jamie whispered, "That sounds like someone cranking a pencil sharpener."

Tom thought he heard chalk screeching on a blackboard as he stood frozen to the spot. When the sounds quieted, the three found their way back to the classroom they had visited earlier. The overhead light illuminated the scene. The desks stood upright. The books from the shelf lay open on them.

"It must be an English classroom," Rich told the others. "Look at that big poster. It says, 'An example of a simile: I just washed my hair. It looks like Angel Flake coconut, all white and curly.'"

On the board, under TODAY IS OCTOBER 31, 1981, the lists of names and figures had changed. The only writing on the wall now was: JAMIE TOWNE . . . RICHARD SPENCER . . . THOMAS TOWNE.

"What the—? Who else knows we're here?"

"Did you tell anyone where we were going?"

"How could I? We didn't decide until we were blocks from the A&W! Who could have been in here since we were, before?

Then, in the dead of night, the school bell began to ring up in the roof tower. Not like for a school day. It was more like the slow knell of a church bell. And it tolled on and on and on. That was creepy enough, but Jamie had counted the number of tolls. It rang out enough times to total their ages! Fifty one!

"Wow! That's enough noise to wake the dead!"

"Or our parents—or the sheriff or any one else in town."

"But how did it ring? Someone had to pull the rope in the main entry!"

They started moving cautiously in case someone else was in the building and intended to do them harm.

In the lights from the cars pulling into the circular driveway, the kids saw Pat, a former custodian—almost a fixture of the school—up in the stairway balcony to the bell tower. Everyone knew he had been dead for forty-some years. What the people of the ghost town didn't know was that he still came back at night, without pay, to look after his building and protect it from vandals. He hated the mess they made. He always straightened up again at night, swept the floors, and had things ready for the teachers when they came the next morning.

"He must even write their lessons and lists on the board for them," Jamie whispered.

Tom added, "And now that he's done his work once more, he can ring the bell and announce a new day."

They huddled in the front entry and watched. But moments later, when their anxious parents met them at the front doors, there was no custodian to be seen. Just Rich and Tom and Jamie and their parents, who heard the bell ringing, checked their clocks, and found that their teenagers weren't home yet from work. And the sheriff and a few others showed up, awakened by the bell that had for so many years also called them to school.

From that Halloween night on, the hundred or so citizens of the ghost town seemed to respect the abandoned schoolhouse more than before. And Jamie, Tom, and Rich never walked by it again after work.

Butcher, Baker, Candlestick Maker

MAYBE MUSICIAN, MORTICIAN, FURNITURE MAKER? Presumably it could have been any of the above who haunted the D.B. Searles Building in St. Cloud in the early 1990s.

Ann S. Kim, intern staff writer for the *St. Cloud Times*, linked Colbert's Funeral Home with the ghosts that reportedly inhabited the building in recent years. In her June 30, 1998, article about the landmark building, Kim wrote that the funeral home was the "longest-lasting tenant" of a whole group of them that followed the original occupants.

The three-story pressed-red-brick structure no doubt made an impressive sight when it went up in 1886 to house the German American Bank. Kim noted that Dolson Bush Searle, a lawyer, had financed the construction after attending law school and after moving farther west.

Above the main-floor bank, original occupants included insurance agents and lawyers. Above their quarters, on third floor, was the Masonic Temple.

By itself, the fact that the funeral home eventually processed many bodies in that same structure does not unquestionably establish that the ghosts are related to the funeral parlor's doings. Other earlier inhabitants included a motor company's advertising office personnel, members of a musicians' association, a piano tuner, and employees of a furniture store. Customers and clients of any of those might be as responsible as the corpses handled at Colbert's. Isn't it possible that the spirit of a tailor, tape measure trailing, might visit his former location

92

now and then, to be comfortable in his former haunts? Or that a violinist might return in spirit in an attempt to recapture a lost melody?

Colbert's Funeral Home was located in the building between 1940 and 1970. Later, Jeff and Holly Celusta operated a popular restaurant there called D.B. Searle's. They closed their business in April 1998. The new owner, Tom Emer, remodeled the restaurant to prepare it for an August 24, 1998, opening.

Through the years of food preparation and service, waitresses have reported incidents they call spooky. Ann S. Kim wrote about a waitress who, in 1991, "felt her hair pushed down by an invisible hand or fingers" when there was no breeze. Though she saw no one who could have done it, "the expressions on the onlooking bartenders' faces confirmed that something strange had just happened," according to Kim.

On another occasion, an employee was sure he had put out all the candles on the tables. He knew as well as anyone that he had to make sure they were all out before he closed up for the night. Yet, after he had extinguished all of them, he noticed that the candles in one section were again giving off their wavering light.

In a conversation with the new owner, even more recent "spooky happenings" came to my attention. He said, "I witnessed some of these myself, and others were reported by the waitresses."

It took very little prodding for him to tell about the ghostly incidents.

"Here's one thing that happens," he said. "While there is no visible operator in the elevator, it goes up and down as though someone were in there, pushing the buttons. Seeing that happen gives me a real eerie feeling.

"Another puzzlement is how the chairs get turned around from the way we left them the last time we moved them to clean, or just to straighten up. It's weird. We have it all done, the way we want it, and all of a sudden everything's reversed.

"Julie, one of several dependable waitresses, had a funny feeling one night when she was putting away some glasses that had just been washed and dried. No one else was near them, and they were sitting off to the side of the counter in the table service area. While she watched, some of the glasses shattered. And once a light bulb in the ceiling shattered for no apparent reason, and we had to pick the shards of fine glass out of the carpeting.

"And these weren't just figments of a new waitress' timid imagination. I saw these things happen, too."

Perhaps patrons who again fill the booths and tables at D.B. Searle's will experience such unexplainable happenings. Possibly the live patrons of the year 2000 and beyond will experience a creepy, crawly feeling late at night in certain nooks and corners when the presence of an occupant from the previous century slips past.

Heavenly Choirs

DORA LIVES IN AN OLD WHITE FRAME HOUSE that has been improved sometime in the past. Her parents had lived there for a few years before she moved in with them. Then, as her parents grew older, she looked after them.

Things started moving the day after Dora's father died. She never knew what would move next, or where. First it was a plate on the kitchen counter. Then a glass on the table. Then an ash tray slid across the coffee table top.

Dora really had plenty to do to complete the funeral arrangements, clean the house for company and be ready for callers. Yet within those few days before the funeral, objects kept moving before her troubled eyes. When she started checking for logical reasons, she found no moisture under the glass, no slant to the counter, no reason for the ash tray to scoot across the coffee table top. She decided this was one of those situations that called for an emphatic confrontation. She said loudly, "Go away! Leave me alone! I have work to do. I don't need this, too!"

Whatever it was left. And the funeral was conducted peacefully, with no upsetting incidents.

Some time later, Dora's mother died. A week after the funeral, Dora sat in the den reading the paper with Poco, her dog, on her lap. Poco wasn't very big. That's why he was named Poco, making use of a musical term for a little bit of anything, like a little more lively, a little bit slower, or anything else in small amounts. Poco, small to begin with, did grow, but only a little, by small degrees, gradually.

95

While Dora read her mother's obituary, Poco suddenly got up and jumped down off her lap. He looked toward the living room and wagged his tail as if he recognized someone who had just come in. He joyfully welcomed the visitor. Dora was dumbfounded. No one had knocked. She'd heard no one come in, and she saw no one by the door. But Poco went into the front room and very carefully walked around a spot as if someone was standing there. Then he pawed at the invisible guest's ankles, begging for attention. Dora saw no ghost, but Poco acted exactly as he always had when Dora's mother returned from her walk.

The strangest incident was somehow connected with a photograph and the people in it.

Dora has a large, framed, black-and-white photo of her parents. She had hung it in the living room at the time of her mother's death. She thought it would be nice for the relatives to see them there on the wall.

After the funeral, Dora heard music in the evening. Yet she had nothing playing. At first, she thought maybe the neighbors had their stereo volume set high. Or maybe some neighborhood kids in the neighborhood drove past with their car radio turned up. The music got louder and louder. Dora went out on the porch, only to find there were no cars. She heard no music coming from the other houses in the block. She went back in to see if her own radio had been left on, but it wasn't. She even unplugged the TV. The music got even louder. Then it stopped.

This thing with the music happened several times over a month or more. Once, Dora called her sister in another county to let her listen to the loud music over the phone. Elizabeth couldn't hear it. Dora tried to tape it, but the elusive strains managed to not be recorded. The more Dora heard the music, though, the more familiar it became. She couldn't recognize the compositions by name, but it dawned on her that she was hearing beautiful organ music with its moving crescendos, like that she had heard when she played recordings of the Mormon Tabernacle Choir or a similar group.

After a couple months, Dora decided to rearrange the furniture in the living room. She hung her parents' photo in another room. The music suddenly stopped.

After a while, Dora had the thought to put the photo back where she'd had it at the time of her mother's funeral. She wanted to see what would happen. She tried it, and she heard the music again. The moving strains were nice to hear, but disturbing, too.

A natural question directed to Dora after listening to her story was, "Did music play a significant part in your life earlier or in the lives of your parents?"

Dora slowly answered, "Well . . . yes . . . but I'd never thought about that. I did sing solos for a time, mostly patriotic songs for conventions and other group meetings. And . . . before that . . . I sang at the top of my lungs, walking to school and back. I guess I started singing when I was five. And Mother whistled and Dad sang as they went about their work on the farm. My sis and I always knew just where they were. We felt a closeness in the family when we heard their music.

"Yes, now that you have me thinking about it, music was a noticeable part of our lives. Not just mine, but the whole family's. Now, I wonder what the connection could have been between the photo and the music. Do you suppose my father, who loved to sing and who died first, didn't want to leave his wife and daughters, so he hung around and let us know he was there by the sweet strains of heavenly choirs?"

To Host a Ghost

A THREE-STORY HOUSE IN THE EAST ISLES neighborhood of Minneapolis has a long and interesting past. Most of the homes there are older, built between 1900 and 1920, some of them on land purchased from the United States government in the mid-1800s. Many of those properties changed hands numerous times before someone finally built houses on the lots.

The house that figures in this story has been "home, sweet home" to more than one ghost. It was built in 1904. Nearly a dozen owners were named on the abstract between the time of its construction and the time when Jack and his wife purchased it and moved in. They liked the location, within walking distance of the Lake of the Isles. They liked the fact that it was in a quiet neighborhood with lots of families and children, and, though the house was ninety years old, it was well built. They liked several unique features of the nearly century-old house. They thought they could enjoy living there.

Once the packing to move and the subsequent unpacking to settle in were done, they felt at home in their newly acquired home. As the flurry of activity calmed to more of a routine broken by seasonal tasks, Jack found time to clean up the maple leaves from the previous fall still lying in the front yard.

As he raked the leaves to bag them, an elderly man walking by paused and looked up at the house. "Name's Henry," he said as he extended a hand. "Lived here in the middle o' the 1960s. Rented a room upstairs from the widow who owned the house then."

98

Putting his rake down, Jack invited the man in. "Would you like to see the house as it is now?"

"I'd be much pleased t'do that, sir. It's been a long time . . . over thirty years already."

As the two moved from room to room and floor to floor, Henry commented on changes. "This'n here was my room," he said as they entered a room on the second floor. "It looks 'bout the same . . . no big changes here."

The two finished looking into the second-story rooms. Then they climbed the narrow stairs to the attic. When Jack flipped the light switch, Henry commented on how nicely finished and furnished the attic was. "And not as dark as it usta be when I lived here."

Looking more closely at the furniture and the floor, Henry recalled that in the old dark attic, he had often heard rapping sounds. He said, "Them sounds led me t' conduct seances up here through the two years I lived here. Sometimes I heard the voices of spirits. Never was sure whose. Think maybe I was in contact with the spirit of my father some of them times. The other folks called him Walter. But I don't hear or feel anything like that now. I knew the house was haunted. I had some int'resting times here."

Jack said later, "He didn't go into detail and tell me about them before he left the house and walked on."

Another day, Jack was taking out the trash when another man stopped by. Jack thought he had seen him around a few times. The man introduced himself as "old Jacob."

Old Jacob said, "I actually owned this house during most of the 1970s." Jack invited him to come inside and look around.

Jacob accepted, and he spoke of the improvements he had made to the house. He told Jack, "I installed the leaded glass windows myself. Got 'em cheap, too. The folks updating the house next door didn't see the beauty of their leaded glass windows, so I bought them for little or nothing and made use of them here.

"Another neighbor, older than anyone on the block, used to throw some pretty wild parties down the street a ways. My daughter and I used to meet a ghost in the hallways of this house after some of those parties. We'd see that ghost pretty often, usually in the upstairs hall at the back of the house. Just for fun, we called him Tipsy, for 'the tipsy ghost that partied too long.'"

Jack asked Jacob if he had any idea whose ghost that was. Jacob, thinking he might have said too much already, answered hesitatingly, "No-o-o, but you needn't worry about it. The house probably isn't haunted any more. The ghost seems to have moved with me to where I live now. And that's five good, long blocks from here."

Jack later met a person who had formerly lived next door. That person reported, "People who lived in your house for a while spoke of unusual sounds, photos being moved, footsteps in the attic."

At that comment, Jack felt a little left out because he had not been privileged to meet the ghost that so many others had met. But he thought it must have been a benevolent presence, since he and his wife had not been bothered. He concluded that an earlier owner might have discouraged the ghost by a long process of renovation that took place in the attic. He thought the former presence felt uncomfortable and left.

Jack and his wife kept in mind what the two former occupants of their house, as well as the former neighbor, had said. They thought it would be interesting to host a party in their home for any of the earlier residents they could locate and perhaps hear about the other spirits who once had haunted their house.

"Who knows?" Jack said to his wife. "With all the changes in the area, they might even be looking for a place to call their own. The spirits, that is . . . not the people who used to live here."

No Child's Nightmare

RENAE J. ANDERSON SHARED THE DETAILS of incidents from near Granite Falls. She said, "When I was in elementary school, we lived in a large farmhouse southwest of Danube. I shared the southwest bedroom with Toni, my younger sister. She and my older sister, Deb, and I have each had at least one strange thing happen to us in that bedroom over the years.

"As for me, something made me wake up one night. I sat up in bed. When I looked over toward the doorway, I saw the outline of a figure. Unlike the build of members of my family, this figure was tall and broad enough to fill the door frame.

"Not knowing who or what I was seeing or what might happen, yet knowing it was no child's nightmare, I hid under the covers. Nothing else happened then . . . or if it did, I wasn't aware of it.

"A few years later, after I moved into a different room in the same house, Toni occupied that southwest bedroom alone. On many mornings she would get up to find things moved around on her dresser, things such as photos, jewelry, knick-knacks, money, her hair brush—her personal belongings. None of us had ever moved them, but just knowing about it gave us a really eerie feeling when we were in there. We were never sure if we were entirely alone.

"About four years ago, Deb came down from the Cities to spend the weekend while her husband was on a business trip. She brought their infant daughter along. For some reason, perhaps because the baby was fussing,

101

Deb woke up one of those nights. When she looked toward the end of the bed, Deb felt that someone was there. As she looked, the end of the bed sagged as though someone had just sat down. Deb could also feel a pull on the blankets from the weight of someone sitting there. As I had done earlier, she just hid under the covers and tried to get back to sleep.

"Our two brothers haven't said anything about similar experiences in that room, but then they haven't spent that much time in what was usually 'the girls' room.'"

Renae had another story to share. These incidents happened in a house twenty miles west of the large farmhouse near Danube where she lived as a girl.

As Renae said, "Strange incidents come to mind for this house, things that happened since we bought this place in February of 1998. Just two or three months later, I woke up a few minutes before my alarm would rouse me so I'd get to work on time. I thought I could hear two-year-old Jonathan calling for me from downstairs. Since he's an early riser, I just thought he woke up and went right downstairs to find me. I went to the stairwell and called for him to come up and go back to bed. I didn't want to go down to look for him because it was so early and all the lights were still off.

"I didn't hear anything, so I called out again. I was just about to go down to look for him when I heard a sound from Jonathan's room. I turned, and . . . sure enough . . . there he was, just coming out of his room, rubbing his eyes as though I had wakened him. But I was sure it was his voice I had heard calling to me from downstairs.

"As I turned to check on four-year-old Andrea, I heard someone go down the back stairway at the end of the hall. Andrea's room is right there by that stairway. I thought maybe my husband, Bryan, had gone down the back stairs to get Johathan. But that wasn't it. Bryan was still asleep in our bed.

"I figured it was Andrea I had heard going down the back stairs, because one-year-old Danica couldn't get out of her crib by herself yet. I hurried down the hallway. Before I went downstairs, I glanced into the girls' room. Andrea was sound asleep.

"I knew I had heard the wooden steps creak under the weight of someone or something, and in a descending sequence. When you use a stairway a lot, you notice the sounds the steps make and you get used to them. Though this house is almost one hundred years old, there are no new creaks because the house doesn't do much settling anymore.

"My husband, Bryan, works a different shift than I do, and he watches TV when the rest of us are sleeping. The next night, Bryan told me he had heard me calling out while he was watching television. His TV room is at the bottom of the front stairway. He closes the eight-foot-tall solid wood door at night to muffle some of the sound of his surround system and not wake the rest of us. When he's watching TV, if I want to say something to him, I have to be standing next to him, and I have to speak very loudly or even yell. He said that when he heard me call out, he yelled, 'What?' but I didn't answer, so he came up to see what I wanted. When he did, I was asleep.

"Bryan didn't think it was anything to be alarmed about, until I told him I had heard someone calling for me, and I told him about the footsteps I'd heard going down the back steps. Then we both felt a little shaky.

"Nothing else unexplainable has happened here in the time we've lived in this house, except sometimes I hear sounds upstairs. But now if I think I'm hearing one of the kids calling to me at night, I stay put and wait for them to come to my room for me.

"We tried to find out if anyone had ever died in this house. We'd heard that a ghost sometimes lingers, especially if someone has met a tragic or violent death. We think that the house may have been built for a doctor, or at least occupied by one. It may also have been owned by a lawyer, possibly the doctor's son. Once we found medical files from the turn of the twentieth century in a niche under a stairway. Then we found medical books as well as law books, up in the attic. The last names written inside the fronts of some of the books were the same. We found that the house was later rented to others, usually older folks, retired couples, some singles, for about forty years. We've been told that it was rented to families for a short while, but not usually, and we wondered if the fact that we were a family with several children had anything to do with why we had a ghost in the house now.

"How these bits of information we've gathered all tie in together to explain the sounds and the callings in the night is still a mystery, but we don't feel threatened because none of us have ever been disturbed much by them, and none of us have been hurt. It makes us wonder, though, what it's all about."

A Swinging Red Lantern

FARMERS REPORTED SEEING A MAN swinging a glowing red lantern and walking on the Omaha Railroad tracks south of Le Sueur. Neighbors said someone lived in a cave in the hollow along the road to Ottawa. Young couples out for a moonlight stroll didn't loiter long.

It was generally thought that the man with the lantern haunted the area. But no one wanting to communicate with him could approach him successfully. When they tried, he disappeared. Whoever it was, he became known as the Le Sueur Brewery ghost.

The area was Old Brewery Hill. John remembered his father and other old-timers talking about the "spirit," and John kept the story in mind for many years. He said it went way back to when the brewery burned down.

According to Tom Conroy's account in the *Le Sueur News-Herald* of November 18, 1986, George Kienzli started the brewery about 1875. Kienzli put up a small building and dug two cellars into the hills. He used large wooden casks in one of these to age the beer. He packed ice into the other one to cool the beer in warm weather.

Several men worked for Kienzli. They brewed the beer each week, and they hauled it to Arlington, Henderson, and Le Sueur. Near the brewery, cattle were fattened on the by-products.

After Kienzli, two others bought the business. Neither of them operated it long before it was closed. But just east of the Ottawa road, the remains of the cellars can still be seen by those who know which side of which hill to examine.

The building itself burned down, but the stories grew about the ghost that haunted the area. They were retold by Ruth Kinsey in the *Le Sueur News-Herald* of October 26, 1960, reprinted from a 1936 New Ulm newspaper. It was believed that a man lived in one of the caves. People said they saw him come from the cave and, carrying his red lantern, walk on the tracks. But he and his lantern seemed to dissolve whenever anyone tried to catch him.

One of the stories was that he paid no attention to trains on the track nor to their warning whistles. He just kept on walking along, swinging the lantern. Trains sometimes stopped to get his attention. When the brakeman stepped down to get the man off the tracks, there would be no one there. That happened more than once.

The folks in the area were concerned. Someone checked the caves and found some old clothes, a straw tick, a shoe box, and some bones.Yet someone was seen going in and out of the cave again, later on, at night.

For a while, no one wanted to live in the house across from the old brewery site. Later, someone built a new house there, and they said the hollow was peaceful in their time. But others who remember the early stories, even those about hearing noises like machinery running in the cave, walk by quickly. They wonder if they can pass the hill without seeing the man and his swinging red lantern moving on down the tracks or finding his way back to his cave in the side of Old Brewery Hill.

Not Ready to Go

When Percy went to the hospital, his grandfather had been dead for several years. Nevertheless, the grandfather appeared to Percy's wife, Pauline, and announced, "I'm ready to take Percy back with me."

Being a spirited woman, Pauline spoke up. She said, "No, you don't! He's not ready to go yet!"

Later on, when Percy died, Pauline had to attend to all the usual details. She and son Doug visited with the other mourners and accepted their condolences during the serving of the lunch. Pauline told the ladies in charge where the floral arrangements and potted plants should be given. Finally they could go home.

While Pauline followed Doug across the porch, she was thinking that the house would be quiet and that for a time it would be a relief. Once inside, she put her purse and gloves down on the little table in the hall. Then she started toward the living room. That was when she screamed.

From the next room, Doug asked, "What's wrong?"

Pauline gathered all her courage to answer him. Even then, her voice trembled. "Well . . . looks like . . . your father . . . beat us home. He's . . . standing in the front room."

Doug had a hard time believing that, so he looked, and he saw his father there, too.

Percy kept coming back now and then. He had one stiff leg, so when he was there, the family could easily recognize him by the sounds he made going up and down the stairs. He would skip every other step. That made the stairs easier.

107

Once upstairs, Percy would enter the bedroom where he'd slept before he took sick. There he just sat and rocked, and he came and went as he pleased.

One day Doug brought an antenna downstairs. He planned to put it on the car. It was one of those ten- to twelve-foot whips, and Doug's mother cautioned him, "Be careful, son. Don't mark the ceiling with that."

In the next moment, it must have been Percy's ghost that bent the flexible top of the antenna down so it wouldn't do any harm.

After a while, Pauline gave her son the hutch that Percy had used to display his collection of miniature farm animals. He had always kept these figures on the shelves in a certain pattern, without variation. That way, he knew just where each one should be, and he could tell immediately if any were missing.

It soon became Doug's wife's duty to dust the hutch. When she did, Dorothy rearranged the animals three times to suit her own tastes. She hardly thought it would hurt to move them around a little since she had to move them anyway to dust. But each time, Percy's ghost came during the night and put them back just as he had left them. As he did this, Dorothy could hear the sounds of the animals being moved. She found it hard to sleep soundly once she figured out what was happening.

Finally Doug told his wife, "You'll learn to leave Dad's animals alone." And now she does. When she dusts, she puts each animal back just where Percy apparently wanted it.

After a time, Doug's mother married again. Her second husband's name was Ray. In their home, in the kitchen, Ray sometimes felt an extraordinary chill. He believed it was the signal that Pauline's mother, as a spirit, would come to visit. Moments later, the family could recognize the fragrance of her favorite perfume.

One day Ray drove his pickup to a distant place, but it seemed he was not alone. The scent of Pauline's mother's perfume accompanied him in the pickup for the whole day's ride.

Ray said, "I didn't think it was any more strange than this story about a house near the A&W root beer stand in Worthington. They say a woman died in the house. Then the man who owned it rented it to a young couple. Sometimes they left their dishes in the sink and moved on to things they'd rather be doing. During the night, and first thing in the morning when they woke up, they'd hear a lot of clattering in the kitchen. When they went out there for breakfast, they'd find the dishes done and in their places in the cupboards.

"I think," Ray concluded, "there must be some spirits that take pleasure in making life more pleasant for the living."

'Round About Stearns County

MEMBERS OF THE STEARNS HISTORY MUSEUM located and offered several examples of "legends and lore" from the area. These are mostly from the colleges in the St. Cloud area, where the first granite quarry was worked in 1868, thereby blessing St. Cloud with its nickname "Granite City" of which this is said: "Busy, gritty Granite City."

One story has to do with an object rather than a person, though several persons observed the phenomenon and felt its chilling effects.

About twelve years before the time of this writing, a group of young monks had gathered for what they considered a serious meeting. Just in case the discussion became long and drawn out and perhaps dry, a pitcher of water and a tray of glasses were provided. While the pros and cons of the matter at hand were aired, and while each gentleman in turn spoke his opinion while the others listened intently, suddenly the calm atmosphere was broken by a strange occurrence. The pitcher of water lifted from the table. That drew everyone's attention. But that wasn't all. As the men's eyes nearly popped from their sockets, the pitcher, still filled with water, floated around the deathly-still room three times before it fell, broke, and splashed its contents all over the floor. No one who watched it happen could think of any logical explanation.

That happened at St. John's University. Not far away, in the Collegeville-Avon area, there is said to be a haunted farmhouse. Some years ago, strange things started happening there after the owner of the house walked home from town one night on a bet, though no one seems to remember what the bet was all about. He didn't make it to his farmhouse—at least, not alive. It was late, and it was winter. He fell asleep and froze to death in a snowbank.

Many years later, occupants of that farmhouse would waken at night to see a man's face hovering in the bedroom. They heard voices calling from out in the yard. Sometimes the residents heard their dogs barking and growling as though they had been frightened, but there was no clue as to what had roused them. Inside, in certain rooms of the old house, very cold drafts were felt from time to time, but no reasonable cause such as an open window or door was ever discovered.

On North River Road near the old Heim's Mill is another site that seems to be haunted. The mill, originally Arnold Mill built by the Arnold family, later became Heim's Mill. It was restored and is still in operation at the same place. In fact, in the year 2000 the Heim's Mill people plan to celebrate the 100th anniversary of their acquisition of the mill. It still grinds grain but is no longer water powered; it uses electricity. However, as a historic site, formerly the work place of many oldtimers, it provides reason enough for reports of hauntings.

Near the mill, folks have reported hearing strange sounds—sounds that in themselves are fairly normal but that defy explanation when someone tries to check them out. For example, sounds of vehicles running, doors slamming, house doors opening and closing, bookpacks being tossed onto a porch, but no one can ever find or see the person or persons responsible. Folks in that area are puzzled as to what made the sounds they've heard.

As is the case at many colleges and universities these days, there is a Lutheran Campus Ministry House at St. Cloud State. No one has been able to prove it, but it seems there is an unusual presence sometimes lurking on the stairs of that building. Students have wondered if it might be an angelic presence.

That presence might be easier to accept than another—the reported presence of a ghostlly cat. It was said to be "living" with the owner of a book store and her real, very much alive cat, Garfield. When the owner knew exactly where Garfield was, she sometimes sensed another cat walking around on her bed in the night. "That," she said, "was really spooky, especially since I never felt another cat's footstep once I turned the lights on. They just stopped dead in their tracks, whatever made them in the first place."

Moving Woes

WHEN JOHN AND LUCY MOVED from Mankato to Worthington, they settled into a split-level house. Lucy indicated later that she could sense a presence there, almost from the first.

Lucy said, "Our bedrooms were on the upper level. We kept a night light in the bathroom. Sometimes in the night, when one of us would get up to use the bathroom, the night light would be off, but a hall light would be on downstairs. We didn't really need that hall light on, so we weren't in the habit of turning it on when we went up to bed. Yet, it would often be on.

"After a few similar incidents, we concluded that there must be someone else around, too. Someone we couldn't see. 'Maybe a ghost,' our daughter said.

"We joked about it at first, but then such weird things happened that we began to take it seriously.

"In addition to our bedroom, the upper level had two connecting bedrooms with a half-wall partition between them. We used one as a girls' room, and the other for the boys.

"One night John, Jr., was sleeping in his room. He woke up to feel the pressure as of someone sitting on the bed and creating a tug on the covers. The next morning, once he was up and had come down to breakfast, he asked his sister Judy what she was doing in his room in the middle of the night. She said, 'I wasn't in your room. Why? Did you think I was walking in my sleep or something?'

"John, Jr., described what he had felt. Judy said, 'Well, it wasn't me!'

"That incident was a little scary, but John, Jr., doesn't scare easily. He said, 'I didn't even open my eyes. I just rolled over and groaned, and whatever or whoever it was went away.'"

Lucy continued to tell her story. "I remember that a while after we had first moved in there, those little happenings became a bit annoying. I finally took someone's suggestion and confronted the ghost. I said, and I wasn't a bit timid about it, 'Hey! Maybe you were here first, but we have to live here, too, and we might just as well get along!' It was pretty quiet for a while, then. Nothing else happened until we started moving.

"As it turned out, that house we were renting was sold, but we found another house just a few blocks away. Its nearness made it easy for us to move a load at a time with our pickup truck. We proceeded to get the other house ready to move into, and we got busy packing our things up for moving them.

"It seemed that the presence that had been living among us didn't want us to leave. When we had everything packed up from our closets and cupboards, along with other smaller items from all over the house, we stacked and loaded all the boxes we could easily handle. That was everything except for the heavier furniture and large appliances.

"That was when eerie things started happening again. When Judy came to help, she always spent the night with us. Late one night, I woke up to sounds as if someone was sliding the hangers back and forth on the rod in the downstairs closet where we kept everyday wraps like jackets and coats. Judy heard the sound, too. She said the next day, 'Someone must have been trying to keep me from sleeping, with all that jingling and jangling of hangers.' The thing is, we had already taken everything out of that closet, except for the hangers. We had no clue as to who had been playing with them.

"One time," Lucy went on, "the screen door through which we went as we set the boxes out, ready to be loaded into the pickup, was squeaking. That was in the night, too, and Judy and I both heard it. It squeaked as if someone was swinging it back and forth, open and shut. We checked the door first thing in the morning. It was still hooked. We asked each other who had unhooked it and then hooked it again before morning. No one had."

Finally, John and Judy had loaded the last boxes into the truck. When John slammed the endgate in place to fasten it, he found it very hard to do, but he did get it latched. Lucy was already over at the other house, but commented later that she never could fasten it by herself; it was just too hard to do. And she knew that the people who bought the pickup later said it was the toughest endgate they had ever tried to manage.

Well, even if the endgate was securely in place, closed, a small antique chair from the front end of the pickup box tumbled out over the endgate and broke on the street.

Lucy recalled, "When John was ready to drive that load over to our new home, he remembered that our son Bob and a friend were going to move one other load of odds and ends from the basement level and the garage that night, but they hadn't arrived yet. Judy wasn't planning to hang around and wait for them. She said, 'I'm getting out of here!' and she came on over to the other house. I was already over there. A little while later, John thought of leaving word for Bob as to how we could be reached. He wrote a note and went back in the house to lay it on the kitchen counter. No one bothered the note, so Bob and his friend found it all right. But John said later that he had a real funny feeling when he went in with the note. He said it felt just like someone stood close behind him. 'I felt my hair stand up on the back of my neck. But I saw no one at all in there! It's my last memory of that house and the eerie feelings associated with it.'"

Eerie Sounds

WHEN GREG LIVED ON WESTERN AVENUE in St. Paul, he experienced sound and motion that left him with a creepy feeling. He recalled, "I would hear sounds no one else heard. For instance, once I was sitting in my pickup in the parking lot at 204 North Western, with the windows open. I don't remember now why I was sitting there at 2:17 A.M., but I heard a gentle moan nearby. I heard that eerie, gentle moaning several times as I sat in my truck. It was usually summertime, and I was usually outside when I heard it, but once I heard it during early spring, while I was in my basement apartment. That time, I heard it through closed windows.

Once I was sitting in my truck near Virginia and Dayton, kind of listening for the sound. I heard it almost directly behind me, as if it came from just over my shoulder. Yet, when I looked, there was no one there. I continued to be aware of the sound as it moved west on Dayton Street, but I could see nothing to account for it, and the sounds didn't disappear immediately.

"This has been going on for a while, usually in early spring or early summer. Sometimes I hear sounds that are almost explosive, but then they go away. In 1994, I was leaving my current building after delivering papers, when I heard the sounds "explode" over my shoulder. Sometimes they seem to be coming from a block or a block and a half away. Once, they seemed to move toward me down Selby Avenue while I sat still, motionless.

"There was a time when I delivered papers on Summit Avenue. On some of those early mornings, just

116

the temperatures were cold enough to chill me through, but as I sat in my truck reading parts of the paper, I would hear conversations. This happened more than once. Sometimes it was a little more like a mumbling or a muttering in the background. In June or July of 1995, as I again delivered papers in the early morning hours, I heard the sounds sort of explode right above me. Sometimes it was more like a conversation about whatever was going on in the area, such as when the first historical house to be sold on Summit Avenue was up for sale. That's when I heard conversations about what was going to happen, but saw no one nearby talking about it. That was really weird. I knew what was happening, but not who was talking about it.

That Cathedral Hill area in St. Paul is known for several homes of well-known early residents: railroad promoter James J. Hill, novelist F. Scott Fitzgerald, druggist W.A. Frost and others near Western Avenue and Selby. It makes me wonder if the spirits of some of those prominent historic figures still inhabit the area, and if they do, why?

Besides being puzzled about the sounds, I had another problem. I often lost my keys, but always found them again, sooner or later. I couldn't be sure if I had misplaced them, of if someone or something else was responsible. Just recently, though—to be specific, it was on August 15, 1998—I lost them "officially," maybe permanently. Since then, I haven't heard those sounds."

Annie Mary's Restless Spirit

IN ALBIN TOWNSHIP IN THE SOUTHERN part of Brown County, the story of Annie Mary's restless spirit is known by many.

Annie Mary died when she was six. Her grave is on what was her parents' farm, the old Twente place, about eighteen miles southwest of New Ulm. It's just west of Hanska and a little farther northwest from Madelia. Robert and Karen Fischer were the owners and occupants of the farm when this story surfaced.

There has been some disagreement as to the cause of Annie Mary's death. Some say she fell from a hayloft soon after her sixth birthday, was injured and didn't recover. Some say she had scarlet fever and slipped into a coma, causing her parents, Richard and Lizzie (Elizabeth) Twente, to believe she was dead.

However, the Brown County death records indicate that Annie Mary Twente, the second of five girls, died of a natural cause—"lung fever"—on October 25, 1886, at age six. Lizzie Twente's foster granddaughter, who lived at Willmar at the time this version of the story was written, was told by her mother that Annie Mary died of diphtheria.

In 1886, the death of a child was not terribly unusual, whatever the cause. Neither was the location of Annie Mary's burial site. Many early settlers buried their dead on their own land. But the duration of her first interment was unusual, if one believes the stories.

One part of the legend is that Annie Mary's mother, Lizzie, felt that they might have buried their daughter alive. When the grave was opened, the inside of the coffin supposedly showed signs of a struggle. There were scratches. Annie Mary's face, which should have been fixed in repose, was instead fixed in terror and her eyes were wide open. She had reportedly torn out a clump of her hair in her deep despair. According to the tales, the body was definitely not in the same condition it was in when it was placed in the coffin.

Numerous news staff writers have retold the story, at least twice in Halloween issues in 1979 and 1980 and once in June, 1986. But then, Annie Mary's birth in 1880 and death in 1886 both occurred in October. Articles were printed on the hundredth anniversary of her birth and death. Readers recall seeing the story in the *Mankato Free Press*, the *New Ulm Journal*, the *St. James Plaindealer*, and other papers. The legend's details were provided by news writers, the Fischers, and their neighbors. The Brown County Historical Society filled in some of the facts.

One of the articles gives credit to the late Art Guttum for information about Annie Mary Twente's first burial site. Though Guttum died early in 1989, he had farmed near the old Twente place. He told a staff writer that the little girl was first interred in the Iberia Cemetery, but her father didn't approve. Perhaps his reason was that it was in Stark Township, too far north. Or perhaps he could already tell that the cemetery was fast becoming abandoned. So Richard Twente chose a place in the corner of his 160 acres, which he had purchased in August of 1884 for $1,140. He moved Annie Mary's coffin to the chosen spot, on the highest point of his land overlooking the farm. In 1914 the farm was sold to the grandfather of Robert Fischer, and the little Twente girl remained buried there.

It could be that the legend speaks of the grave being opened because Richard Twente moved its contents from the cemetery to his own land. Guttum said that after Richard Twente buried his daughter for the second time, he put up a wooden fence around her grave. That didn't satisfy him, so he had a plasterer help him build an eighteen-inch thick, four-foot high wall of stone and mortar. They installed an iron gate with a brass lock. Neighbors remembered seeing the gate and lock as they drove by on the old wagon trail between Albin Township and its neighbor to the east, Lake Hanska Township.

The key to the gate's lock was found many years later, among the possessions of one of Annie Mary's sisters. That sister was Elizabeth, born four years after Annie Mary. Elizabeth's foster daughter, also named Elizabeth (Thissen), still had the key at the time this story was written. But it seems the gate and the enclosure could not contain the spirit of the young girl buried there.

The story is that when the gate is open, her restless spirit dressed in white wanders on the hillside in the moonlight. They say that car headlights suddenly fail as people drive by the enclosure. Two young boys who visited the site one night reportedly had a frightening experience. One climbed the tree near the wall, lost consciousness and fell. He had to be taken to a hospital. It is said that doctors could not explain what was wrong with him.

Other tales are told, such as that on hot days, the stone is cold and vice versa. Others tell that cars stall on the bridge nearby, horses refuse to cross it or are spooked there, and the ground just in front of the marker is barren. But there used to be a peony bush that bloomed every spring for Annie Mary and her family.

The tombstone of gray granite has been broken from its base. As the saplings grew, their roots pushed up under the marker and tilted it. The black iron gate is gone, but the hinges are still in the wall. The enclosure is overgrown with weeds and grass and brush, and it's often littered with empty cans and paper trash. The wall itself is cracked, and moss has begun to form a mosaic over it.

Perhaps Richard Twente once thought the plot would also become the burial place for himself and his wife. There was enough space. A tree was planted on each side of the entrance; one, an ash, still stood a few years ago. The other is merely a charred stump. Though there are signs of wear, the inscription on the stone can still be read. It says, "ANNIE MARY / Born / Oct. 14, 1880 / Died / Oct. 26, 1886 / Father and Mother, May I meet you in your royal court on high. / Twente."

Stories about Richard Twente's unusual personalitiy have perhaps added to the legend. When he brought his family to Brown County from Kentucky, his religion was different from that of his neighbors. That may have caused them to see him as very strange. But they soon found that he was also brilliant and enterprising; for instance, he sold nursery stock. In 1918 he wrote and copyrighted a pamphlet about planting fruits and fruit trees.

He was very strong physically. He built a large, three-level barn with a stone foundation, by himself with only the help of his wife and girls. For a long time, it was the biggest barn in the area. In the mid-1880s, he built a granary that was for many years listed on the National Register of Historic Places. It had a scale for weighing, a hoist and belt system, and seven bins on the upper levels. And Twente put up a two-level hoghouse, also with help from his wife and living daughters.

But Richard Twente also did some strange things, according to the people who know the legend. Once he started across the prairie in a sled, taking his wife and daughters with him. The only reason he turned back was that his wife begged him to, so they wouldn't all freeze to death. Some say people were afraid of him because of his fits of anger and his extreme strength.

Once, he left his family and went to Canada where he bought some "worthless land." Before long, he contacted his wife and tried to borrow ten dollars from her "to buy bread so I won't starve."

Robert Fischer, who grew up on the old Twente farm, said that Richard Twente dug up Annie Mary's body twice. Once, it was because he thought the corpse might have been stolen.

Richard Twente died around 1920 while he was in Canada cutting or hauling wood. His riderless horse went to a neighbor's place. When the neighbors investigated, they found Richard Twente had died of a heart attack. He is buried next to his wife, Lizzie, and some of her sisters in the Methodist Cemetery at Raymond. Lizzie had gone to live near there with her daughter Elizabeth for a time. Elizabeth's foster daughter said that Lizzie died in 1936.

Apparently it was someone else who tried to dig into the grave as recently as 1985. Robert Fischer shoveled the dirt back to fill the hole again.

Some who have studied the phenomenon of spirits of the ghostly kind say that ghosts are the dead who are stuck on earth. A spirit may be waiting for something, such as a decent, secure burial.

Annie Mary had a decent burial at least twice. But since her white-clad spirit roams the hillside on moonlit nights, she might have reason to be displeased. Her iron gate is gone, her wall is cracked, thistles form a tangle in the enclosure, and her tombstone is no longer intact.

A pastor of the Lake Hanska and La Salle Lutheran churches once asked Fischer to think about having the grave moved, once more, in an attempt to avoid the disrespect and vandalism at the site. Perhaps, if that were done . . . or if the wall and tombstone were repaired . . . or if the gate were located and once again hung on its hinges and closed . . . and if the key were turned in the brass lock one final turn . . . perhaps, then, the restless spirit of Annie Mary Twente could rest peacefully.

Not Just a Dream

SOMETIMES A HAND RESTING on one's shoulder is comforting. Sometimes it's . . . surprising.

Mrs. Alex Walker of Magnolia in Rock County was Aunt Minnie to her family. Since she was a sister to Georgette (Mrs. G.O. Bigelow) who lived in St. James, she was Aunt Minnie to Georgette's daughter Lois (Mrs. Clayton R. Johnson of Worthington).

About thirty-five years ago, the Johnsons were visiting friends in Rochester, Minnesota. One morning at the breakfast table, Lois recalled a dream she'd had the night before. Though it's hard for her to remember the details so much later, she does remember that her Aunt Minnie appeared. She was sitting in a chair in the same room with Lois.

"I put my hand on her shoulder for a few seconds," Lois told those around her, "and I asked her, 'How are you, Aunt Minnie?' It seemed so natural, because I knew she hadn't been well.

"Aunt Minnie's answer surprised me. She said, 'I've come home to die.'"

The others around the table were surprised, too. Mrs.Walker had been in a care center at Mountain Lake, between St.James and Worthington. Though she hadn't been well and had been there for a while, death was not expected at the time.

After Lois told her dream, she said, "After all, it was only a dream. Nothing like this has ever happened to me before. Let's not let it shake us up. We must have been talking about Aunt Minnie last night before we went to bed."

123

Later that morning, the Johnsons left the home of their Rochester friends to return to their own home in Worthington. On the way, they stopped in St. James to see Lois' parents, the Bigelows. The first thing Mrs. Bigelow said when Lois and Clayton greeted her parents was, "Aunt Minnie died last night."

Samantha

SAM HAD COME TO BE ACCEPTED by the family that lived in the large, two-story square house in a town in Jackson County. This family needed the spacious home more than did the previous occupants, who had inherited it from the original owner, a business man who built the house in the early 1900s. His wife had died in one of the four upstairs bedrooms. She was quite elderly and had been ill for some time.

When the current family bought the house in the late 1950s and settled in, the oldest daughter, Peggy, at age eleven took her pick of the bedrooms. Her choice was the northeast room. Her two younger sisters, six and four at the time, were told to take the room across the hall. That left a bedroom for their parents, a guest bedroom, a study, and a bathroom all on the second floor. And so, who would have which room was settled. For a while.

Elaine and Judy weren't happy with their room. They felt something strange about it, and they were frightened. They said it was way too cold all the time, even though it was the beginning of summer when they moved in. Their room also seemed dark or crowded, to them. Elaine said later, ". . . like sitting in a chair recently vacated by someone else, the person's presence still lingering."

Then the noises started. At first, the family thought they were the normal sounds of an old house settling or the loud cracks sometimes heard when the outdoor temperatures dropped quickly.

"But eventually," Elaine said, "we all had to admit to hearing the measured thump of feet on the stairs and the occasional clang of a pan being filled with water in the basement.

"As time passed," she continued, "I graduated to the room across the hall, leaving Judy in 'that room,' as we all referred to it. We were in our early teens, and though teenagers' perceptions of reality and fantasy can be questionable, we did know the difference between what was reality and what was something else. We had taken to calling the presence 'Sam,' short for Samantha. And she became most active during the years 1967 to 1974."

The girls' father told of the first really frightening experience the youngest daughter, Judy, had. "She woke up one night," he said, "feeling someone shaking her bed. She saw a woman standing there. She knew it wasn't her mother. She saw a fairly slender woman with long, light hair—a little wavy on the ends. She had large, dark eyes and seemed to be wearing a long, light— maybe white—dress. The woman stood there and looked at Judy. Judy felt afraid and started to say something, but the figure disappeared. After it was gone, Judy wasn't afraid anymore. She felt unbelievably calm, considering."

Sam's appearance always happened when Judy was upset or concerned about something. When she felt Sam sit down on her bed and she could see the bed "go down" on that side, she was calmed by Sam's presence. When she stopped worrying about her problems, the sag in the bed came up again, and all returned to normal.

Sometimes, Judy said, the presence actually touched her. Instantly she was calm and able to go to sleep again.

Elaine told about other happenings in their home. Some evenings the window shades all snapped up at the same time. Pictures fell off the wall in unison. The heavy furniture and marble-topped tables would be spun askew in the middle of the night.

Elaine remembers most vividly a night when she was seventeen, and Judy was fifteen. Their parents had gone out for the evening. When the girls finally settled down to the business of getting to bed, the shade snapping and clattering and general noise started up in Judy's room. After a while, Elaine heard Judy say in a loud voice, "Knock it off, Sam. Go to Elaine's room."

A second later, Elaine felt the air in her room move. Elaine recalled, "It was cooler and carried a scent of flowers. Nothing happened beyond that, and I eventually drifted off to sleep. I awoke hours later in the grip of the most acute terror I had ever felt. The edge of my bed dipped down as if someone had just sat down on it. I felt a cool hand on my forehead, followed by an almost liquid-like calmness. It was just as my sister had described it: cold terror, then something as soothing as warm water—a pervasive gentleness.

"I sometimes wondered if Sam's appearance left a door open for someone unpleasant, and Sam had to take care to remove that other presence.

"At any rate, I got used to feeling Sam's closeness, like another member of the family, almost. Sometimes I said, 'Sam, go back to Judy's room.'"

Judy told about her most frightening experience. It happened when she was in sixth or seventh grade. She awakened in her room, that same northwest room, one night. Things didn't feel right. The room was very cold. Then she saw a man standing at the foot of her bed. He wore a tall, black hat and dark clothing, but he had no face. Judy had the inexplicable feeling that someone was extremely angry. Then Samantha came, and the man disappeared. Again, it was as if Samantha took care to remove the unpleasant presence.

The girls' parents told of times when they smelled perfume. "Sam's identifying smell was pleasant, that of a woman busy in her home, cooking and cleaning. This all made sense," Elaine told, "since we believe she is the spirit of the lady for whom the house was built, who raised her family there, and who died there, in that bedroom that was Judy's for so long."

There were many times when members of the family turned to take a second look at a shadow. But one summer, when Elaine was visiting friends in another state, her father walked down the upstairs hall late one night. As he went by Elaine's bedroom, he passed someone. He thought at first it was Elaine, but then realized she wasn't home. He quickly looked into her bedroom, but there was no one there.

Elaine claims that when Samantha is seen, "There isn't real substance or form, but rather a suggestion of shape, an impression of gender, a feeling. Apparently it is a similar impression to the one I leave. Dad thought he saw me that night he first saw Sam."

Guests of the family have experienced Sam, too. One young man who came to visit was put up overnight in the guest room because a blizzard had come up and delayed his leaving. In the morning, he said that someone had rattled the doorknob in the night. He said he opened the door, but no one was there. Later he heard it rattle again. He got up really fast once and looked out in the hall. He heard someone walking up and down but couldn't see anyone. The young man never visited there again.

Another guest came to visit Judy one winter. Again, when it was time for him to leave, traveling was out of the question. He was put up in the guest room. Just after he went to bed, he felt something hit the bed. The bed went down. Then he felt pressure on his chest. He thought the family's fifteen-pound Manx cat had landed on him. When he found out in the morning that the cat had been in the basement all night, he learned to accept Samantha as the ghost in the house, almost a member of the family.

One summer, the girls' father woke up to feel someone holding his right hand. It was a warm and soft grasp, but firm, too, like the palm of another hand, just clasping his. He thought, I must be dreaming. He looked at the wall to see shadows of tree branches with their leaves, moving in the light from the street as usual. He noticed that the window was open. He wasn't dreaming. Just as he tried to grab the hand to look at it, it slipped out of his hand and disappeared. He turned to see that his wife was sound asleep beside him. No one else was there in the room. He wasn't frightened, though. He said it was a comforting hand.

His wife's experiences are different. She'll suddenly smell something like a delicate fragrance. "It's pleasant," she said. "Sometimes I smell it when I wake up at night. It's there for a while. Then it's gone. I can't pin it to anything. It's not like the others' experiences."

If things disappear, "Sam's been here" is the explanation. Or if something shows up that wasn't there earlier, "Sam must have left it."

One time, just after the girls' mother had just finished a thorough housecleaning, she found a piece of metal on one girl's bedroom floor. It appeared to be part of an old gun barrel, but there were no guns in the house. "And a piece of metal that size could never have escaped my mother's scrutiny," Elaine pointed out.

She also said that articles of clothing had disappeared over the years. Not one sock caught in the washer, but shirts, sets of lingerie, favorite jeans. Elaine said she thought maybe Sam's cleaning schedule didn't mesh with her mother's, and Sam just went on cleaning and straightening up on her own, when she was ready. Maybe she put their clothing in a special place, reserved for her own daughter. Or maybe she had decided to take over the mending.

At the end of one Christmas vacation, when Elaine was ready to go back to school, she and her mother looked and looked for one item of clothing that had been a gift. Elaine wanted to take it back with her. They took time out for lunch. When they went back up to Elaine's room, they both saw the gift in its box, set up on end as if on display in the middle of the floor.

"Oh! Sam again!"

When Elaine and Judy were in college at the same time but in two different states, they were still visited by Sam. Elaine, who had always been the most sensitive to Sam, would get the feeling from Sam that Judy wanted to talk to her. When Elaine called Judy then, Judy was surprised. "Why, no, but let's talk anyway," she told Elaine.

Each of the girls eventually married. Elaine had a family and lived in a city in another state. Samantha seems to have followed her there. In the new home, a key disappeared once, but it was found right where Elaine had looked, where she expected it to be but hadn't been before . . . until Sam put it back.

Another time, Elaine came downstairs to the living room to find the chair near the fireplace rocking. She knew then that Samantha had been there, too.

And Sam goes to yet another state to visit Judy, who still remembers her very cold room at home and the visits from Samantha.

Elaine wonders if Samantha will stay with the family through the younger generation. Her young son has already met Sam. He left his room several times one night when he couldn't get to sleep. The third or fourth time, Elaine, asked, "What's happening? You ought to be asleep by now." He finally asked his mother to get "that lady" out of his room. Then Elaine told Sam to get out, and Sam moved on.

Elaine's husband has also met Sam. When he was talking on the phone one night and Elaine was sound asleep, he heard someone ask, "Who's on the phone?" Puzzled, he didn't answer. He was asked again. The third time, he just blinked his eyes, and the quizzing stopped. Immediately, Sam was gone.

Judy and Elaine have been aware of Samantha most of their lives and have believed in her. Elaine's personal note was, "We see her as capable of communicating emotion. She seems to be aware of our emotions. We consider ourselves lucky to have someone from another place and time know us and care about us."

No Peace for Mortals

JEAN AND HER HUSBAND woke with a start. "What time is it?" she whispered. Then the living room clock struck two.

"Did you hear something, too?" Al asked.

"Yes. Like a low moaning. I thought I heard someone say 'I'm the man' or something like that."

Jean got up then and walked through the house, listening closely. When she passed the bathroom, she realized the sound was coming from there. It was the children's talking He-Man toothbrush set.

Al took out the batteries, and they both figured that would end the disturbance.

"The next morning, about nine o'clock," Jean said, "I heard the sound again. It seemed to be coming from the toothbrush set, even without its batteries. But it didn't sound like talking now. It was more a low, garbled mumble, as if someone wasn't satisfied with the way things were.

"I threw it in the garbage then. It was just too scary. Later on, late one night, I was wakened by a baby crying. I got up and walked down the hall to the kids' room. They were all asleep, and everything looked all right. But I missed something. The next day, outside, right by the steps, I saw my son's night light. It was a little ceramic shepherd boy with his arm around a lamb. It had been a gift at the birth of our son. But now the little boy's head was broken off.

"At the time, the kids were pretty young. One was still a baby. The other one was about three. I wondered what this was all about. It reminded me of Agatha Christie's *Ten Little Indians*. Was this broken night light

131

a warning that something would happen to one of the family? Was it some ghost sending us a signal?

"Even when I went back to bed, I could hear a baby crying. And we talked about it a lot. Possibily the ghost was connected with a relative's tragic death. The spouse survived, and a very young child suddenly had just one parent. The relative had spent the night on the farm with us the night before the accident."

The next experience seemed to support Jean's theory. "A few weeks after the accident, our infant son's pacifier disappeared. He was really attached to that pacifier, and of course he cried. We looked literally everywhere that night. Mom even came and helped us look. It wasn't anywhere around. Finally we quit looking for it, but the baby didn't quit crying. I think he cried half the night.

"The next morning, when we got up, the pacifier was lying on the floor right by the front door. We had all looked there!"

"We wondered if, as a result of some sudden, tragic accident and death, a ghost could find no peace and didn't want relatives to have peace, either . . . not even the baby. When that thought was verbalized, relatives recalled that pacifiers might not have been an accepted way to comfort a baby in the victim's time. Some thought maybe the dead person was missing a child who had just celebrated a first birthday that month. It also seemed possible that the one who had always been young in spirit before the accident just didn't want to depart this life at such an early age.

Jean finished her story with the report that these incidents have never happened when guests have been present. "The ghost appears only to the family, but not in visible form, more through actions.

"But when family members come to visit the farm where we live and where my family grew up, they have a strange, haunting feeling whenever they walk near it or come on the place. As if none of us will ever be allowed to forget."

Weird Sounds and Windmills

ADELL BARNES, WHO LIVED ON A FARM in Murray County, was frightened by daytime sounds of someone going up to second floor bedrooms. From her bed at night, she heard someone running fast from the north room into the landing which was used as a daughter's bedroom. Then she heard running come into the couples' own bedroom and out through the wall.

One night something walked alongside the bed on Adell's side and then seemed to move through the wall to the outside. She said, "The kids never heard anything. Neither did my husband."

When someone asked Adell if she ever saw anything, she said, "No. I was so afraid, I didn't open my eyes. And I never felt anything either. I just heard the sounds."

At that time, Adell and Charlie had been sleeping upstairs. They decided to move their bedroom down to what had been a dining room. Charlie helped take the bedroom furniture down, and Adell rearranged the clothing and made up the bed again.

One night when they were asleep, Adell sensed someone walking across the foot of the bed, across her feet, back and forth. They didn't have a cat or dog, so it had to be something else. She didn't look, but she woke up wide, and she was sure she had felt the motion. She tried to be brave. She told herself, "Now, this is silly. There's nothing in here going across the foot of the bed."

Just then, she felt something like a hot breath or breeze blowing into her face. She stayed there, frozen in fear, and pulled the covers over her head.

133

Maybe these incidents had such a terrifying effect on Adell because of an earlier experience. When she was a girl of thirteen or fourteen, she and her older sister Bonita stayed home one night on the family's farm in Murray County. Their parents had gone to a dance and wouldn't be back until late because refreshments were always served after the dance at the home of the hosts. Usually they had cake and coffee and a good visit before they went home.

As they left, Adell's father said, "Now, you girls both know you have to turn the windmill off after it has pumped long enough. Take care of it before you go to bed, and don't forget." Fred could be really stern.

About an hour later, the girls went out to shut the windmill off. Back in the house, they had a glass of milk and some soft molasses cookies before they went upstairs to get ready for bed.

Through the open window, they could hear the pump start up again. Pulling overalls over their nighties, they went down again to see if they hadn't secured the handle that shut the windmill off. They knew that when they pulled the lever down, they had to fasten it securely with the heavy wire to the corner support of the windmill frame.

"Maybe we didn't fasten it well enough before," Bonita said as they made sure it was secured this time.

Having had enough of running back and forth in the increasing darkness, they went right up to bed. By now it was at least ten o'clock. The pump made an eerie sound as it started working again. The wheel at the top of the windmill creaked as it slowly started around. Then the blades howled. Exasperated, Adell said, "I'm not going out there again!" And they went to bed and soon fell asleep.

When their parents came home about one thirty from the dance, the windmill was still going. Fred went out to check it and found it wasn't shut off.

Naturally, the girls were in for a scolding the next morning. But after they told their father they had gone out there and secured the lever twice, he was thoughtful and quiet for a while. Then he told them maybe it wasn't their fault, but he wouldn't explain.

Years later, while Adell and Charlie lived on the same place, they were out milking in the barn one evening. They had four children at that time, and Adell, the young mother, was twenty-nine or thirty. As Adell carried the milk to the cooler, a thought came through to her as if someone said, "Your Dad isn't going to be with you much longer." There was no one there, and she heard no real voice. "But the thought came into my mind," she said.

Adell knew her father had been in the hospital earlier, but he'd been discharged with a clean bill of health.

Adell told Charlie, "Grandpa was eighty-five when he died. Dad has a long time to live yet." But her father died on December 29, just a couple months after the warning.

Her father seemed to have a premonition, too, that he would die soon. He said to Adell, "Some day you're going to have to take care of Mom."

One morning at breakfast, Fred and his wife looked again at all their Christmas cards and shared some fudge and coffee before he went out to the garage to leave for work. He usually left the garage door open, but his wife saw later that day that the garage door was shut. When she noticed it, she didn't recall having heard it opening that morning. When she and the neighbors checked, they found Fred dead. He'd had a heart attack.

Contents of a Box

WHEN DONNA AND BILL WENTWORTH moved to a house in rural Nobles County, they noticed something strange. There were no doors between the living room and dining room, just an opening. That in itself wasn't so unusual; many homes had a wide, open archway or a simple wide space in the wall between those rooms. But they noticed it was always cold there. Someone told Donna that an unexplainable cold area in a house indicated that it was haunted, and that the cold spot was the place where the ghost came and went.

Sometimes they felt a sensation as of the wind or a fan blowing their hair at that spot. Many times when the Wentworths were in that place, they felt activity or energy of some kind causing movement of air; yet they found no cause.

Sometimes in mild weather, Donna came in through the back door of the house. As soon as she stepped into the kitchen, she would hear voices. Often as many as five or six men seemed to be talking in the living room. Their voices were jumbled, and she wasn't able to sort out any one voice from what was being said. The sound resembled that of a radio when the station isn't tuned in well. She often went into the living room to turn the radio off, only to find that it wasn't on.

One day someone who had lived in the house earlier came back to visit. When he was told about the voices, he explained them with one comment: "Oh! The card games in the parlor!" But that's all he would tell Donna about the phenomenon.

136

Aside from the voices and the cold and wind in the space between the two rooms, a few more things happened. When Donna and Bill had lived there a couple years, Donna decided it was time to clean out the attic. She was curious as to what was up there. When she had gone in through the small door, she screwed an adapter into a socket and connected an extension cord and a crookneck lamp. All set, she was ready to explore the attic. Suddenly the door slammed shut, the extension cord came out of the socket, and she sat on the attic floor in total darkness. No explanation seemed plausible.

Another time Donna had just gotten up in the morning when, before she went anywhere near the kitchen, she could hear water running. Going to check on it, she found the faucet fully open and water gushing full force into the sink. It took two or three turns to turn it off. She's still wondering how it got turned on.

One day when she sat alone in a rocking chair in the dining room, she heard the steps creak, one by one, as they would if someone were coming down from upstairs. She could see the door at the bottom of the stairway, and she watched it. After waiting for what must have been at least ten minutes and feeling more frightened by the minute, she got up, jerked open the door, and found . . . nothing there!

Another ghostly incident was a visual happening, in winter, with snow on the ground. There were footprints in the snow, and they came to the back porch. They were neither Donna's nor Bill's. There were definite tracks, though, as of someone who walked up to the back door and never left. The size of the prints was normal, a medium size. If they were made by an overshoe, the soles were worn smooth. There was no snow inside on the floors, melted or otherwise. There was just the one short path, starting in the middle of the back yard and continuing to the back door. They saw no backtracking, no doubling of the prints. The Wentworths weren't even using that door at the time; it was secured and weatherproofed for winter.

Before the couple had moved to that house, several other families had lived there. Each family upon moving out had taken all their possessions with them, as far as anyone else knew. But one day Donna noticed something she had never seen before. The closet under the stairway to the second floor had an overhead shelf just above the door space. She hadn't noticed it before, and neither had her husband. The shelf was just a little above head height, and not in the direct line of vision as they entered the closet and looked straight ahead. That day, though, Donna noticed it and got a stepstool so she could reach the shelf.

She found a flower box. The printing at the end of the box indicated it came from Ludlow Greenhouses, an early business in Worthington. Donna read, "LUDLOW GREENHOUSES . . . LUDLOW BROS., PROPS. FLORAL DESIGNS A SPECIALTY . . . DELIVER WITHOUT DELAY."

Donna and Bill found out that Ludlow Brothers Greenhouses had operated from about 1916 to early 1944. Milton, the oldest of the Ludlow brothers, and H. Dwight, the youngest, had been the owners. The other brother, J. Burr Ludlow, was a banker and insurance man. Helen Wilson Smith, a long-time resident in the area, remembered when the men made steel frames to go around the glass for the greenhouses that housed all the plants. Smith knew five generations of the Ludlow family. The business had been sold to a Sioux Falls firm long before the Wentworths bought their house.

That didn't help explain anything except the origins of the box. Still curious, Donna took the box down from the hidden shelf to a table near a window where the light was better. In the box were various objects, and she took them out one by one. She thought mementos . . . or souvenirs. If mementos, she thought to herself, they were meant to either warn or remind. If souvenirs, they were merely remembrances, objects saved as a pleasant reminder of days gone by. Among other things, she lifted out a violin, a man's Gillette razor, a bundle of letters, and a wool vest. The razor was in its original package as if ready for a first shave whenever needed. What seemed hard to believe was that all those other people had lived in the house and no one had removed the box or the items in it. Not sure what to do with it, she put the box back on the shelf.

Thinking about the shiny, new razor, Donna started to remember something. She had been told when they moved in that one of the earliest families to live in the house had a sad experience. A son had died at a very young age, either in the house or in a hospital while the house was his home. In fact, the time connected with his death would fit into the time span the Ludlows operated in Worthington. She didn't know what to do with the items in the box and chose just to leave them where they were.

A long time later, two men came to the Wentworths' door. One of them asked, "Could we see the house and farm? This is where we grew up, as did our younger brother. But he got real sick while we all lived here, and he died before we moved away."

Donna invited them in. In the course of the conversation, she ventured, "There's something funny here, though. Something rather unsettling. Did you notice anything strange about the place when you lived here?"

They both said they hadn't. And it seemed that they didn't want to talk about that any more. They just wanted to see the place. Then they slowly made the rounds of the house and yard, coming again to the porch to say, "Thank you for letting us come. You won't be bothered anymore."

And they weren't. Nothing else happened like the earlier events. And the brothers didn't come back. It was as if, in coming that one time, they had released the spirit of their brother who had died young. It seems he had stuck around, doing nothing destructive, but just hanging around as if he wasn't ready to leave his home and his treasured possessions when he died.

"And one more detail," Donna added. "The next time I hung my jacket in that stairway closet, the flower box was gone!"

A Friendly Ghost

LUCILLE SAID, "OH, BOB, I THINK I just have to have it."

Bob answered with a question. "Are you sure you want more old junk around?"

This conversation took place before Bob got hooked on collectibles. Lucille had been into them for quite a while already, in the days when there would be only three or four rummage sale ads in the paper at a time.

At this particular sale, Lucille fell in love with an old rocking chair. It seemed to greet her with a built-in personality. It looked as if it would be comfortable, with its back and seat upholstered and its sides open. Because it was also a pretty chair, it was a bargain at $2.50.

Lucille won out, and Bob, resigned, helped her haul the chair home.

They tried it downstairs at first. It was comfortable. Despite its age, if they just pushed it to make it rock, it didn't squeak. But if they sat in it and rocked, it squeaked. The family came to think of it as a nice squeak, as if a friend was always there visiting and rocking. Since it became so close and important, Bob began to refer to it as *the chair*, with emphasis when he spoke of it.

But as more "old junk" found its way into the rooms on the main floor, Bob suggested *the chair* be taken up to the attic. Something had to go. There wasn't room to move around anymore, and their eight children needed a little space to play and grow.

At that time, the family all slept upstairs in their home on Nobles Street in Worthington. Kelly, the young-

141

est daughter, was thirteen or fourteen. Her room was the first one at the top of the stairs. In the far corner of her room was a door to the attic. By tugging a little on that door, one could open it and climb several steps up to the space filled with old chairs, love seats, boxes of high school souvenirs, and other memorabilia. With them, *the chair* took up residence.

Kasey, Kelly's younger brother, was about three when Kelly was thirteen. No one knew that there was any mystery about the house, but Kasey let it be known that he would rather crawl in with Kelly in her big bed than sleep alone in his room.

One night, and only one, Kelly heard *the chair* rocking in the attic. And squeaking. She knew that meant someone was sitting in it, but no one had gone through her room and opened the door to the attic. At least, she hadn't seen or heard anyone. As scared as she was, she couldn't make herself get up to check. Petrified, she was happy to have Kasey with her that night. She stayed in bed and eventually went back to sleep.

Before that, Lucille herself had gone up to the attic one day and had seen the chair rocking. It was squeaking, too. Yet no one visible was sitting in it, and no attic windows were open to cause a draft that would start it rocking. After that day, Lucille never wanted to open the door to the attic stairs, unless there was a support team present.

After Bob began to get interested in collectibles, too, the doorbell rang one Saturday morning. At first, Bob thought someone had come to see a particular item or just to look around. By now, he thought he knew enough about the business to take care of a customer. Three of the girls were home that morning, but Bob beat them to the door. A man and woman stood there on the steps.

The man said, "I used to live here in this house years ago." Further talk led to, "While I lived here, my little brother died when he was eight. He died in one of the upstairs rooms."

It turned out to be Kasey's room, not Kelly's. One of the girls asked the visitor, "Would that explain why Kasey doesn't like to sleep in his room alone?"

The man's only answer was that he'd sure like to come in and have a look around, if they didn't mind.

The girls took him and his companion all through the house, downstairs and upstairs and even through the porches, where some of the collectibles were displayed on shelves and tables. He seemed to enjoy the tour and their chatter about a ghost. The kids had all talked about it for a long time. Lucille didn't encourage that kind of talk, but she didn't stifle it either. By then the family had accepted the ghost in their home even though they hadn't figured out why it was there.

Before the visitors left, Lucille said, "It was nice to talk with you. I'm glad you were able to come and see the home where you used to live. That must be a good feeling, to be able to do that."

The male visitor agreed, and he thanked them for the tour. Before he left, he told them that he was sure they had a nice, friendly ghost and that they shouldn't be afraid of it. He said he thought the ghost felt at home there, and since they had accepted it, they would have no problems because of it.

"In fact," he said, "I wonder if it is maybe the ghost of my little brother."

The Ghost of Deadman's Hill

THE GHOST OF DEADMAN'S HILL is known by those who lived in the vicinity of a farm north of Willmar. The incident that initiated the story happened on Alice's parents' home place.

Alice first heard of the ghost as a young girl in the summer of 1937, when an elderly neighbor came to help turn the hay that a two-day rain had soaked.

That noon, the neighbor, whom the family called "old Joe," surprised Alice and her brother. When Alice spread a rug in the shade of the big American elm tree and invited old Joe to sit down and rest until her mother had lunch ready, he protested. He said, "No one should sit on a grave. Please be so kind as to move the rug."

Alice felt humbled as she moved the rug to the shade of a smaller tree. That was when her brother asked, "But whose grave is under the elm tree?"

The answer to his question was the beginning of a long story. Briefly, the American elm was planted as a living memorial to a runaway slave caught by a bounty hunter. The slave was chained to a fencepost for the night, but he managed to pull the post out of the ground and free it from the fence. Apparently he crept up on the bounty hunter and the two fought it out. The slave beheaded his captor with the bounty hunter's own sword.

As a young boy before the Civil War, old Joe had accompanied his father and others to the same farm north of Willmar on the morning the body of a black man

144

was found near a corner of the front porch. The man had suffered many gashes and was chained to a large log fence post. When the men followed his trail by the blood and the marks left by the post as it was dragged along, they found the body of a second man—a white man—the bounty hunter.

The slave was buried where he died near the corner of the porch on the farm, where the tree was later planted. The bounty hunter was buried on the hill nearby, where his body had been found.

Two more men died on the hill soon afterward. One was the sharecropper who lived on the hill farm near there. The other was the caretaker who had consequently been asked to do the chores for the sharecropper's widow. By then, by the tracks in the snow, it had been figured out that the ghost of the runaway slave had attacked and beheaded the caretaker and the sharecropper in much the same way as he had killed the bounty hunter.

The three deaths that occurred on the hill were soon generally blamed on the runaway slave and his ghost, who became known as the ghost of Deadman's Hill.

Alice and her brother began to piece things together after old Joe told them the story of the ghost. They learned that their mother knew their house was haunted. She never heard the sounds, because she was deaf, but she claimed to have seen and sensed spirits in the house. And items like flatware and coffee cups and frying pans turned up missing. A day or so later, they were returned. Alice and her brother tried to convince their father that ghosts took the items, but he made it known that he held his children responsible.

One night, the two children stayed awake to listen for the ghost. What they heard that night, and every night after that if they stayed awake to listen, sent shivers up thehir spines. First they heard a faint continuous noise coming from the north. This gradually grew louder and closer until it was right outside the dining room window. The sound was like that of an object being dragged on the ground. After it stopped just outside the window, they would hear the sound of chains clinking, then silence for about a minute before they heard more clinking. The dragging sound would start again until it came to a sudden halt just past the corner of the house. The sound never varied, and it always occurred at the same time each night.

"We could have set our clocks by it," Alice claimed. "We talked Dad into listening to the ghost sounds with us several times, but he always claimed the sounds were caused by mice or rats between the walls, or the wind, or something else—never a ghost!

"After World War II ended and building materials became available again," Alice continued, "Dad bought windows, insulation, and siding to redo the downstairs of the oldest part of the house. My brother and I talked about the ghost during the time we were working on the house. Being older then, we knew that although there had been activity on the farm attributed to the Underground Railway, we would never actually find a tunnel, so we had quit looking for it. But we decided that if during the remodeling we heard the same sounds we had been hearing, and if we still heard them after the remodeling was done, there had to be a ghost, not just the wind or something between the walls.

"Needless to say, the ghost of Deadman's Hill continued to make his nightly pilgrimage to his grave."

Alice clearly recalls one incident a couple years later when she was twelve. It was a hot summer night in early August. She and her parents and brother had worked late in the field, shocking grain until it was too dark to see, before they headed home to start chores.

"I lit the kerosene lamp in the kitchen," Alice remembered. "We all had a bite to eat. Then the folks left for the barn to start the milking, taking with them the one lantern that had some kerosene in it. Meanwhile, I went to the shed for a can of kerosene to refill the house lamp and another lantern before joining the folks in the barn. By then it was pitch dark.

"As I started across the yard towards the shed, the night had not cooled off any. When I reached the shed, I felt my way along the row of gas barrels until I felt the smaller kerosene barrel on the far end of the row.

"After filling the can and feeling my way out of the shed, I faced the house. The light in the kitchen window was very dim. I didn't give this any significance at the time because I knew the lamp was almost empty and I thought it was just going out. It did make it harder to find my way, though.

"As I lost sight of the light entirely, there was no alternative but to keep walking toward the house. Very suddenly the air around me changed from hot and muggy to icy cold. The only thing to compare the change of temperature was that it was like walking into the frozen food locker on a hot day. I hurried my steps, and in seconds the air was warm and muggy again. Much to my surprise, the lamp I thought had gone out was still burning.

"As I entered the house, my brother asked me if I heard the ghost go by. It wasn't until he mentioned the ghost that I looked at the time and realized I had crossed the ghost's path as he rested.

"Together, my brother and I listened as the ghost of Deadman's Hill once again finished his nightly journey to his grave."

Old Zeke Was Still Around

PAUL CALLED FROM HIBBING TO SAY, "I heard on the Hibbing radio station that you were looking for ghost stories from around here. Well, I know a man who lived for a time in a house built on top of an old, abandoned underground mine between Chisholm and Buhl. I'll call him Luke.

"Luke was a good man. The area where he and his wife, Miriam, lived when this happened—and that was four or five years ago already—is known to have many underground mines, especially near Chisholm. Chisholm, Buhl, Hibbing, Eveleth—they're all within the Mesabi Iron Range.

"Luke and Miriam have moved since then. It was a really old house they were living in there. Now they have another, somewhat newer home in the country while he works at the Hibbing taconite plant. But he told me this story awhile back, and it has stuck in my memory, even though it just happened that one time, out of the blue."

According to Luke, late one evening, while he was reading from the Book of Revelations just before his accustomed bedtime, he saw what he thought was one of the oldtimers appear. He showed up right in his home, surprising him like all get out. He was dressed pretty much like a miner, and there was dust and grit on his clothes, as if he had just come up out of the tunnels. He wore a hard hat with a miner's lantern attached. In the quiet of the hour, he sort of slipped up gently and easily through the floor as if he was stepping out of an elevator mine shaft.

When Paul heard this story, he was told that, to Luke, the figure looked just like one would expect an old-

148

timer to look. He was sparsely bearded. His eyes were set deep in his wrinkled face. His cheeks were hollow, his hair almost white and thinning.

Luke said, "We called him Zeke from then on, whenever we talked about him. He slipped into the room without a sound. His boots must have been so supple from use that we couldn't even hear his footsteps. Then he turned and went right through the wall. Come to think more about it, he floated more than he walked. He just disappeared."

Luke and Miriam both saw the oldtimer that night. As they talked about it later on, they agreed that he must have thought he was coming up from the mine and heading home at the end of the work day. They never saw him again, but Paul and others who know the story think that Luke and Miriam must have had some pretty creepy feelings while they still lived in their home above that old underground mine, especially at night.

Of Estimates and Guesses

A RECENT TELEPHONE CONVERSATION between parties at Hibbing and at Worthington brought another story from the iron range to the surface.

Paul's father, Albert, was a carpenter. He was not only adept at using the tools of his carpentry trade, he also had to look ahead and put figures together for estimates as to what a job would cost.

After work one day, he sat at his desk long enough to make up an estimate for Elsie and George, who had a remodeling project in mind. Since he would pass their house on his way home, he thought he could save time by stopping there that same evening.

Their back door—the one they always used—was open, though the storm door was shut to keep out the cold. As George asked Albert to come on in, Elsie set three mugs of steaming coffee on the kitchen table, along with a plate of fresh, warm bread she had just sliced and buttered.

Paul said, "From where Dad sat that evening, he could see down the length of the house and through the windows at the other end, to where the front steps and door were. There were lots of those long and narrow homes in rows in that part of town for many years. That was still true of the year Dad had this experience, about twenty years ago now."

Paul said, "Dad told me that the three of them were sitting there enjoying the coffee and the fresh bread. George had just asked Dad if there was any way the total cost of materials for the project could be reduced, when

150

Dad heard someone knocking on that other door at the other end of the house.

"George and Elsie didn't seem to hear the knocking, so Dad interrupted George to ask him if he wanted to take time to answer the knock. George ignored Dad's question. Elsie calmly refilled their coffee mugs and sat down again.

"The discussion about the costs continued. When Dad heard the knocking a second time, he looked toward the other end of the house, but he couldn't see anyone anywhere near those windows or the other door. It made him a bit restless, but he tried to keep his thoughts on the business at hand.

"Finally, they had gone through the figures in detail and both parties had come to a clear understanding of how the totals added up and what alternatives could help cut costs, yet preserve quality and durability as a result of the project.

"As if some explanation or apology were in order, when Dad thanked George for the opportunity to do business with him and thanked Elsie for her hospitality, Elsie mumbled, almost incoherently, 'But what you think you heard must have been some other noise outside somewhere. As for someone being at the front door,' she said evasively, 'we don't use that door.'

"Before Dad went on home—and it was almost dark by then, so he didn't think they would notice—he purposely walked around the other end of the house, to that front door. The old steps were barricaded from the railing on one side to the railing on the other side, as if the steps weren't safe. And the other surprise was that there were no footprints in the snow, other than the ones he himself was making.

"For Dad, nothing ever explained the sound of the knocking he heard that evening at George and Elsie's front door while they sat in the kitchen with him and overlooked it, though Dad had a feeling they were aware of it. Dad sort of guessed that they sensed a ghostly presence but maybe wanted to keep it quiet."

Folks who know the area well—even some of the small, long-time business owners on Hibbing's main street and in other nearby communities northwest of Duluth—speak now and then, somewhat guardedly, of the old houses and stores that are visited late at night and in the early morning hours by an old man who walks through. They say, if they speak of him at all, that they see him "out of the side of their eye," but when they look more directly, there's no one there, and the doors are still closed and locked. Such stories seems to surface about every five years, then are spoken about less and less. Maybe it's because the area holds its stories and its spirits close.

Acknowledgments

Thanks to all who responded to my request for more ghost stories from Minnesota. The time you took to relate your experiences and to answer my questions made the book possible. When requested, names and locations were disguised to respect your wishes.

I apologize to readers who had to wait for the stories from *Ghostly Tales of Southwest Minnesota* (1989) to be available again. That book went out of print, but versions of the stories are preserved in this new book along with whole new stories from all over the state.

Thanks to the publisher, editors, and others who helped shape this final result, and thanks to the staff at Computer Exchange in Worthington, who helped me succeed in putting the entire book on disk.